700029

D0276723

# Finger Food For Babies & Toddlers

# Finger Food

## For Babies & Toddlers

Jennie Maizels

Vermilion

# Acknowledgements

I would like to thank my husband Marcus for his flawless support and endless proofreading and food tasting. I am also grateful to Kate Howlett, Kim and Kate Tolman, Lucy and Niko, Kate Petty and the following friends and their toddlers for being recipe testers: Dawn and Stella, Ness and George, Emma, William and Thomas, and Karen and Isaac. Thanks also to Jean and David for proofreading.

First published in the United Kingdom in 2003 by Vermilion, an imprint of Ebury Press
Random House UK Ltd to

Random House

20 Vauxhall Bridge Road
London SW1V 2SA

Random House Australia (Pty) Limited
20 Alfred Street, Milsons Point, Sydney,
New South Wales 2061, Australia

Random House New Zealand Limited
18 Poland Road, Glenfield,
Auckland 10, New Zealand

Random House (Pty) Limited
Endulini, 5A Jubilee Road, Parktown 2193, South Africa

Random House UK Limited Reg. No. 954009
www.randomhouse.co.uk
Papers used by Vermilion are natural, recyclable products made from wood grown in sustainable forests.

A CIP catalogue record is available for this book from the British Library.

ISBN: 0091889510

Printed and bound in Italy by Graphicom

# CONTENTS

# INTRODUCTION

I am the mother of a very independent-minded little girl called Millie. This book came about because I discovered a way of ending the perpetual mealtime battles I had with her and I wanted to spread the word.

The problem with my little girl Millie was not that she didn't want to eat, but more that she didn't want to be fed. While too young to feed herself with a spoon, she felt too frustrated to be spoon-fed by anyone else. This often resulted in disastrous effects upon herself and my kitchen.

I started to experiment with food that she could hold, such as sausages and cakes, and feed herself without any 'interference'. I began cutting silly shapes out of omelettes, making things in mini pie trays and converting any leftovers from grown-up suppers into croquettes or wrapping them in pastry. At last Millie began enjoying mealtimes again.

Being vegetarian is even more of a challenge, as I had to make sure that she was always receiving a varied and balanced diet. This forced me to be even more inventive (I am particularly proud of my tofu fishcakes).

To begin with, I found that she ate a lot more if she thought I couldn't see her. No showing off, no trying to put food in Mummy's mouth and no 'Look at me spit my food out!' I hid round the corner with a cup of tea, creeping up only to refill her satisfyingly empty plate. Once she had got into the habit of enjoying mealtimes again, I would try to sit with her, showing her that food was a pleasure for me too.

Not only was finger food a breakthrough for mealtimes in the kitchen, it was also a great boon on the move. It made picnics and car journeys far more bearable. A small amount of preparation would save us stopping for unhealthy snacks or junk food. Millie could eat a nutritious meal without a messy and often public scene. I hope this book will help you to overcome mealtime difficulties with your own child, and to convey the message that food should always be equated with pleasure.

# Notes on Equipment

Have fun treating yourself to a few new cooking things, all vital of course. There's nothing like a bit of cookery-shop retail therapy to inspire you in the kitchen.

## Biscuit cutters

Choose fun shapes that you know your baby or toddler will like. Millie has always loved stars, so from a very early age she gobbled up (most) things that were cut into little star shapes. Other shapes, including teddies, cats, hearts, cars, dinosaurs, aeroplanes and gingerbread men, are all popular too.

For babies of 6 months upwards, tiny biscuit cutters are really useful for making fun sandwiches (see page 25), omelettes and toast, etc.

## Bun tin

For making regular size fairy cakes.

## Electric mixer

Indispensable – the cook's best friend for mixing and blending.

## Kitchen ruler

Useful for finding a mug or glass that is the right diameter for cutting pastry to a particular size.

## Measuring spoons

Try to find a set of spoons that's fastened together to avoid having to rummage for them in several places.

## Muffin tray

Ideal for making small quiches, tortillas or muffins. A mini muffin tray is also useful for making fairy cakes in petit four cases.

## Pastry brush

For brushing pastry and other toppings with butter or egg white to aid the browning or binding process.

## Pastry cutters

Round cutters in a selection of sizes, ranging from 4 cm to 8 cm, always come in useful. (When buying a set, look out for those containing both straight-edged and fluted-edge cutters – great for jam tarts, etc.)

## Plastic tubs

Small containers are essential for on-the-move recipes or snacks.

## Plates with dividers

Specially made for children, divided plates are useful for foods served with dips.

## Siliconised baking parchment

Quite different from greaseproof paper, this is completely non-stick and able to withstand higher heat. Suitable for all types of baking.

Notes on Ingredients

The notes that follow pinpoint particularly useful ingredients, and address some of the questions that relate to the production of food.

## Allergies
For children who are intolerant of lactose or gluten, most of the recipes have ingredients which can easily be substituted for alternatives e.g. soya products or gluten-free flour and bread. For those with nut allergies or from allergic families, only one recipe contains nuts as a key ingredient (a cheese straw variation on page 27). It is **essential** to always check the ingredients of products being used to detect the presence of any food your child may be allergic too.

## Breadcrumbs
Essential for coating many finger foods, breadcrumbs are also invaluable for turning leftovers, such as pasta and rice, into croquettes. I freeze them in sandwich bags and use them straight from the freezer.

## Butter
All butter should be salt-free for infants younger than one year and salted or unsalted for children over one year.

## Fibre
Plant foods contain fibre which is important in our diets, however in children, too much fibre can fill them up and replace more nutritious things like carbohydrate. High fibre foods like Bran shouldn't be given to babies and toddlers. Too much fibre reduces the absorbtion of minerals such as iron, zinc and copper. Try and give some vitamin C containing fruits or vegetables with meals to aid iron absorption.

## Genetically modified foods
While I have strong reservations about using genetically modified (GM) foods, I believe that individuals should be free to choose for themselves. Thanks to consumer pressure, most foods containing GM products are clearly labelled, so you can avoid buying them if you want to.

## Oil

Feel free to use whatever oil you prefer or have to hand for the recipes, but note that olive oil is healthier than many, being low in saturated fat and high in healthy monounsaturated fat. However, for deep-frying it is better to use a thinner oil, such as vegetable or sunflower. Added fat provides a valuable source of energy in children's diets, especially for vegetarian diets which are naturally low in fat.

## Organic foods

I buy organic whenever possible, but as with GM foods, I believe that doing so is up to the individual. Whatever you opt for, remember always to wash fresh ingredients before cooking them.

## Pulses

Lentils do not need soaking. I normally cook them as instructed on the packet (for about an hour) in a little stock to increase their flavour. However, other pulses, such as dried soya beans and chickpeas, need soaking overnight before cooking. Using tinned pulses and beans is a good time-saver for busy cooks.

## Salt

During weaning and under the age of one, no salt should be added to foods. Beware of processed or ready-prepared foods which may be high in salt, such as ready-made sauces, gravies, stocks and salty foods like Marmite.

## Vegetarian alternatives to meat

Quorn ™ has had a bad press recently because some alleged allergic reactions have been reported. I tend to think that many foods can provoke an adverse reaction in somebody. As a vegetarian I feel it is a delicious alternative to meat. It is very adaptable and very useful. I always have a stock of Quorn ™ mince, fillets or chunks in the freezer.

**Tofu,** also known as beancurd, is usually sold in blocks, which can be frozen. After freezing and defrosting, it becomes more porous and readily takes up the flavour of marinades. Grated, it makes a fabulous alternative to minced beef.

# Store-cupboard Essentials

If you take care always to have a selection of fresh vegetables available, you can easily make a meal using some of the following save-the-day items.

Breadcrumbs (see page 14)
Dried mixed herbs
Passata
Soy sauce
Tinned beans (cannellini, kidney and mixed)
Tinned chopped tomatoes
Tofu (you can buy long-life packets)
Tomato purée
Vegetable stock powder

## Superfoods
These are foods that have qualities to help fight illness and promote health, while having no drawbacks. They include nutrient-packed foods, for example apricots, berries, avocados and tomatoes.

## Note
● All spoon measures in recipes are level unless stated otherwise.
● For accuracy, please follow metric or imperial measures only, not a mixture of both.

# First Finger Foods

From around the age of 6 months, babies are generally ready to start experimenting with finger foods. When your child reaches this stage, there are (as you probably know) some basic guidelines to follow.

**Allergies** are commonly linked with certain foods, which should not be introduced until your baby is 6 months old. The usual offenders are cow's milk, eggs, fish, nuts and wheat. It is always sensible to wait three days between trying new foods in order to detect any allergic reaction. If you do notice one, wait a month before trying the food again, and seek medical advice.

**Honey** should be avoided as it contains spores that, although harmless to adults, can cause food poisoning (botulism) in babies.

**Salt** should be avoided for the first year because your baby's kidneys are not mature enough to deal with it.

**Supervision** is **essential** when babies are eating. It is important that they are never left alone because of the risk of choking and gagging at this early stage.

These early months are the time for experimenting and encouraging your baby to discover the enjoyment of mealtimes and eating in general.

Finger food for children under 12 months is a great way of developing their hand-to-mouth coordination and overall dexterity. It nurtures their desire for independence, allowing them to make their own decisions, and leads on, we hope, to finally being able to feed themselves.

# Fruit

The softness and natural sweetness of fruit make it an ideal introduction to finger food. The following fruits are the best ones to begin with.

**Apple**
**Banana**
**Cherries (stoned)**
**Grapes**
**Kiwi**
**Mango**

**Melon**
**Papaya**
**Peach**
**Pear**
**Strawberries**

Fruit should be peeled, cored and cut into hand-sized pieces for babies. The skin can be left on for older children once they are able to bite and chew really well. Beware of choking with fruits like grapes and cherries and never leave your child alone when eating.

Place a small amount in front of your baby: it's better for them to ask for more than to be inundated

# GOOD THINGS

- All fresh fruit is high in vitamin C.
- Papaya and mango are regarded as superfoods, being rich in antioxidants, soluble fibre and vitamin E, which are all vital for healthy body cells.

• Best eaten fresh. Not suitable for freezing.

• Make a taste chart of all the foods you would like your baby to try, noting the date tried and their reaction.

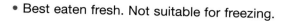

## Vegetables

Holding the warm vegetable fingers suggested below will be a new sensation for your baby, and a great introduction to new textures and flavours. The following vegetables are the best ones to begin with.

**Broad beans**
**Broccoli**
**Brussels sprouts**
**Carrot**
**Cauliflower**
**Courgettes**

**Green beans**
**Parsnip**
**Potato**
**Peas**
**Pumpkin**
**Sweet potato**

Peel the root vegetables and cut into fingers.

Break broccoli and cauliflower into small, baby-friendly florets before cooking.

Steam or boil until soft.

Toss the vegetables in a little salt-free butter if desired.

Peas and broad beans may be crushed slightly, as babies seem to find them easier to eat that way.

# GOOD THINGS

- Carrots are rich in carotene, an antioxidant believed to help protect against cancer and heart disease.
- Green vegetables are very high in vitamin C and zinc.
- Vegetables are essential for a healthy body and mind. They are packed full of essential vitamins, minerals and trace elements.

- Cover and refrigerate for up to 1 week. Freeze for up to 12 months.

- Freeze prepared and ready-cooked vegetables in one-portion variety bags.

# RUSKS

Home-made rusks are much healthier than shop-bought rusks or other teething biscuits. Even if you add sugar, it is a tiny amount in comparison to that in commercial products.

**Makes about 20**

225 g (8 oz) plain flour
½ tsp bicarbonate of soda
1 tsp cream of tartar
50 g (2 oz) softened butter

25 g (1 oz) caster sugar (optional)
50 g (2 oz) yoghurt
65 ml (2½ fl oz) semi-skimmed milk
½ egg, beaten

Preheat the oven to 180°C/350°F/Gas mark 4.

Sift the flour with the bicarbonate of soda and cream of tartar.

Cream together the butter and sugar (if using), then gradually stir in the flour.

Using your hands or an electric mixer, work the mixture until it resembles breadcrumbs.

Combine the yoghurt, milk and egg, then add to the flour mixture, stirring until a dough is formed. Knead the dough a little with your hands.

Take a walnut-size piece of dough, roll between your hands into a finger shape, then flatten using your palm. This ensures that babies can hold them easily and get them into their tiny mouths.

Place the rusks on a greased baking sheet and bake for 20 minutes. Lower the temperature to 120°C/250°F/Gas mark ½ and cook for a further 15–20 minutes until the rusks have dried out.

Remove from the oven and place on a wire rack to cool completely before serving.

# GOOD THINGS

- The yoghurt, milk and egg content of the rusks provide a good dose of calcium and protein.
- These rusks are a good source of carbohydrate, which is important for your baby's energy levels.

- Store in an airtight container for up to 1 week. Freeze for up to 6 months. (To defrost, wrap in foil and bake at 160°C/325°F/Gas mark 3 for 15 minutes.)

- Take the rusks out of the oven after the first 20 minutes of baking for soft-centred toddler treats – delicious with butter.

# Breadsticks

Always firm favourites, breadsticks are a classic finger food and very easy to make.

**Makes about 30**

**450 g (1 lb) strong white or wholemeal bread flour**
**1 x 7-g sachet fast-action yeast**

**pinch of salt (optional)**
**50 g (2 oz) butter**
**4 tbsp olive oil**
**200 ml (7 fl oz) water, at room temperature**

Preheat the oven to 200°C/400°F/Gas mark 6.

Mix together the flour, yeast and salt (if using) in a bowl.

Melt the butter and pour into the flour with the oil and water. Mix to form a firm dough.

Divide the dough into about 30 pieces and roll into pencil shapes as long as your hand.

Place the sticks on a greased baking sheet, brush with a little oil and bake for about 20 minutes.

Transfer to a wire rack and allow to cool completely.

# GOOD THINGS

- Being low in fat and salt, breadsticks are much healthier as a snack than crisps and similar savouries.
- Wholemeal flour is a good source of fibre.

- Store in an airtight container for up to 2 days. Freeze for up to 6 months.

- Store in an airtight container for up to 2 days. Freeze for up to 6 months.

Sandwiches cut into tiny shapes always seems to delight babies: they are easy for them to hold and will usually be devoured with glee. For each of the following filling suggestions you will need 2 slices of bread and mini biscuit cutters (see page 12) to make about 6 little sandwiches.

## Marmite Sandwiches

(Please note: Marmite is not suitable for under ones)

**½ tsp butter**                    **½ tsp Marmite**

Mix the butter and Marmite together in a bowl. Spread on two slices of bread, sandwich together and cut into shapes.

## Spinach and lentil sandwiches

50 g (2 oz) frozen spinach,
  defrosted
1 tbsp cream cheese

$\frac{1}{2}$ tbsp lentils, tinned or
  previously cooked
$\frac{1}{2}$ tbsp grated Parmesan
  cheese

Mix all the ingredients in a blender.
  Butter two slices of bread, spread the lentil mixture on top, then sandwich together and cut into shapes.

## Egg mayonnaise sandwiches

1 hardboiled egg yolk

1 tsp pasteurised mayonnaise

Combine the egg yolk and mayonnaise in a blender until smooth.
  Butter two slices of bread, spread the egg mayonnaise mixture on top, then sandwich together and cut into shapes.

## GOOD THINGS

- Butter is a useful source of vitamin A, which strengthens the immune system.
- Marmite, a yeast extract, is a top provider of B vitamins, which help maintain a healthy nervous system, promote growth and improve energy levels. (Please note: Marmite is not suitable for under ones)
- The lentils and cheese provide a quantity of protein equivalent to that in meat.

- Refrigerate in an airtight container for up to 2 days. Not suitable for freezing.

- Sandwiches are readily portable, making feeding baby whilst out and about far less stressful.

# Cheese Straws

These cheesy fingers are a soft and crumbly introduction
to new tastes and textures.

**100 g (4 oz) plain or wholemeal
flour**
**50 g (2 oz) butter, diced**

**75 g (3 oz) Cheddar cheese,
grated**
**1 egg, beaten**

Preheat the oven to 200°C/400°F/Gas mark 6.

Mix the flour and butter together using your hands or an electric
mixer until the mixture resembles breadcrumbs.

Stir in the cheese and egg, forming a dough.

Roll out the dough to a thickness of 1 cm ($\frac{1}{3}$ in) and cut into fingers,
or shape into thin rolls.

Place on a greased baking sheet and bake for 10 minutes.

Transfer to a wire rack and allow to cool completely.

# GOOD THINGS

- Butter and cheese are good sources of calcium.
- Cheese and eggs are also high in protein.
- Wholemeal flour is a great source of complex carbohydrate.

- Store in an airtight container for up to 1 week.
  Freeze for up to 6 months.

- Try replacing 25 g (1 oz) of the flour with the same
  weight of ground nuts to provide extra zinc and
  protein.

# Dips and Dippers

Toddlers love to feel that they're doing something all by themselves – something grown-up and exciting. It promotes their independence, asserts their individuality and is great for their hand-to-eye coordination and general dexterity.

Millie got the idea of dipping quite early. ('Dips! Dips!' was one of her favourite mealtime chants.)

The trick is not to overwhelm toddlers with choice: a small serving of dip and a limited selection of things to dip is preferable to a large array.

Most of the following recipes provide a complete meal, so they don't have to be regarded just as snacks. And remember – there are many other recipes in this book that can double up as dips or dippers (see pages 24 and 39, for example).

One last point: a beginner-dipper is not a neat one, so try not to worry too much about mess.

# Dippers

Bread fingers are obvious choices as dippers, but vegetable sticks are also ideal for dipping too.

**1 pitta bread or 1 slice of bread**
**1 tbsp olive oil**

**small selection of raw vegetables, e.g. carrot, celery, courgette, cucumber, green beans or red or yellow pepper**

Preheat the oven to 180°C/350°F/Gas mark 4.

Brush both sides of the pitta or bread with olive oil and cut into fingers about 2 cm (¾ in) wide. Place on a baking tray and bake for about 5 minutes until they are crisp and hard.

Wash all the vegetables, peel or prepare as necessary, then cut into finger-length strips about 1 cm (⅓ in) in diameter. Arrange a small selection of veg and bread on a plate with your chosen dip and serve.

# GOOD THINGS

- Bread is a valuable source of carbohydrates, and is high in fibre and B vitamins.
- Cooking vegetables causes them to lose a lot of their vitamins, so serve them raw as often as you can.

- Store in an airtight container in the fridge for up to 1 week. Not suitable for freezing.

- Raw button mushrooms, broccoli and cauliflower florets are also popular dippers with young children.

# Guacamole

The subtle flavour and lovely green colour of this dip appeal
to all generations.

**1 small avocado**
**1 tsp fresh lime juice**
**3 cherry tomatoes, finely**
**chopped**

**1 tbsp crème fraîche or**
**yoghurt**
**salt and freshly ground black**
**pepper to taste (optional)**

Peel and stone the avocado and mash in a bowl.

Add the lime juice, tomatoes and crème fraîche. Mix well and season
to taste.

# GOOD THINGS

- Avocado is known as a superfood because it contains a wealth of
  vitamins and minerals, especially vitamin E, which help reduce heart
  disease and is believed to lower the risk of cancer.

- Cover and refrigerate for up to 3 days. Not
  suitable for freezing.

- Guacamole can also be used as a sandwich
  filling. Combine with cheese and ham for an
  interesting variation.

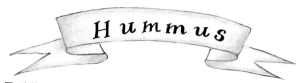

# Hummus

Toddlers love the nutty flavour of this favourite dip.

**1 tin chickpeas, drained and washed**
**1 small garlic clove, crushed**
**½ tbsp tahini**
**juice of half a small lemon**

**pinch of cumin**
**pinch of salt (optional)**
**1 tbsp yoghurt**

Mash the chickpeas using a potato masher, or whiz to a purée in a food processor.
Add the rest of the ingredients and mix until smooth and creamy.

# GOOD THINGS

- Chickpeas are rich in potassium, which is important in controlling the balance of fluid in our bodies and also iron which is essential for carrying oxygen in our blood. They are also high in folic acid which is important for healthy cells.

- Pour a little olive oil on to the surface of the hummus to prevent it drying out, cover and refrigerate for up to 3 days. Not suitable for freezing.

- Hummus makes a good sandwich filling, and tastes great with chopped tomatoes.

# Creamy Dips

The following simple dips go especially well with the Chicken Nuggets and Vegetable Crisps on pages 44 and 79.

## Cream cheese and herb dip

50 g (2 oz) cream cheese
½ tbsp crème fraîche or natural yoghurt

1 tsp finely chopped herbs, e.g. basil, coriander, chives or parsley

Mix all the ingredients together and serve.

## Creamy Tofu dip

50 g (2 oz) smoked or plain tofu
50 g (2 oz) yoghurt
1 tbsp olive oil
½ tsp lemon juice

salt and freshly ground black pepper (optional)
a few snipped chives
1 tsp fresh or dried dill
1 tsp paprika (optional)

Whiz all the ingredients in a mixer or food processor until smooth. (The paprika will make the dip a pretty pink colour, but it is not essential.)

## GOOD THINGS

- The cream cheese and crème fraîche are high in calcium, which is good for teeth and bones. Vitamin $B_{12}$ is important for carrying oxygen in our blood and is the only B vitamin not found in plant sources.

- Cover and refrigerate for up to 1 week. Not suitable for freezing.

- If you're really pressed for time, you can make a quick dip by mixing pesto or tomato sauce with mayonnaise.

# Home-made Ketchup

This is very useful for encouraging children to eat foods that they would not normally eat. Be warned, however, it is quite addictive.

**400 g (14 oz) tin tomatoes or passata**
**1 tsp balsamic vinegar**

**1 tbsp tomato purée**
**2 tsp golden caster sugar**

Liquidise the tomatoes, then place them in a large saucepan. Bring to the boil on a gentle heat, then reduce to a simmer.

Add the remaining ingredients and cook steadily for about 15 minutes, allowing the mixture to reduce by about half.

Allow to cool, then serve.

## GOOD THINGS

- Tomatoes are rich in vitamin C, which is an anti oxidant and also helps in the aborption of iron from food.

- Refrigerate in an airtight container for up to 1 week. Freeze for up to 12 months.

- Store in a squeezy bottle so that toddlers can have fun serving themselves.

These are my toddler's favourite things to dip – so easy to make and so much appreciated. They're also a great success at kiddies' parties.

| selection of vegetables, e.g. aubergine, beetroot, | butternut squash, carrot, celeriac, parsnip, | potato, pumpkin, sweet potato oil, for brushing |
| --- | --- | --- |

Preheat the oven to 180°C/350°F/Gas mark 4.

Peel the vegetables and chop them into holdable chips. (Carrot, parsnip and sweet potato tend to shrink a little, so cut these slightly larger than the others.)

Blanch the potatoes, celeriac and parsnip in boiling water for 3–4 minutes.

Meanwhile, spray or brush some oil onto a baking sheet and heat in the oven for a few minutes until really hot.

Drain the blanched vegetables, tip them out onto a clean tea towel and pat dry.

Arrange chips on the baking sheet and brush with a little more oil, making sure each chip has a good coating.

Bake for 20–25 minutes, or until golden, turning halfway through the cooking time.

When cooked, pat off any excess oil with kitchen paper and cool.

## GOOD THINGS

- As these chips use a small amount of oil and have no added salt, they are much healthier for your toddler than shop-bought varieties.
- Potatoes are a good source of energy in the diet.
- All fresh vegetables contain vitamins and minerals that make a valuable contribution to your child's diet.

- Cover and refrigerate for up to 1 week. Freeze for up to 4 months. (To reheat from frozen, wrap in foil and bake in a moderate oven for 15 minutes.)

- As a special treat, cut shapes, numbers or letters out of potato slices cut 1 cm ($\frac{1}{3}$ in) thick.

# Hot Dips

For a warming meal, try some of these dips as sauces with rice, pasta, chicken, Fishcakes (see page 45) or Schnitzels (see page 60). Alternatively, serve with some cooked vegetable fingers.

## Warm Bean Dip

210 g (7½ oz) tin cannellini
  beans, drained
1 heaped tbsp crème fraîche

1 tbsp finely chopped fresh
  coriander or 1 tsp dried

Warm the beans in a pan with 2 tablespoons of water.
  Mash the beans thoroughly. Then add the crème fraîche and coriander and mix together well.
  This dip makes a great addition to the burritos on page 59.

## Tomato and Couscous Dip

40 g (1½ oz) couscous
60 ml (2¼ fl oz) salt-free
  vegetable stock

2 tbsp home-made Italian
  tomato sauce (see page 56)
  or passata

Place the couscous in a heatproof bowl. Pour the stock over the couscous, then cover and leave for about 5 minutes until all the liquid has been absorbed.

Stir in the tomato sauce or passata and serve.

## Cheese Sauce Dip

120 ml (4 fl oz) milk
22 g (¾oz) butter
1½ tbsp flour

25 g (1 oz) mature Cheddar
cheese, grated

Put the milk, butter and flour into a saucepan, place over a medium heat and whisk continuously until the mixture starts to bubble and thicken.

Stir into the corners with a wooden spoon, then whisk again for a couple of minutes.

Remove from the heat and stir in the cheese until melted. Cool slightly before serving.

## Warm Aubergine Dip

1 aubergine
1 tsp crème fraîche or natural
yoghurt
1 tsp fresh or dried mint or
parsley

salt and freshly ground black
pepper, to taste (optional)

Preheat the oven to 180°C/350°F/Gas mark 4.

Prick the aubergine all over with a fork and place in the centre of the oven for 30–40 minutes or until a skewer passes through the aubergine easily.

Cut in half, scoop the flesh into a bowl and mash with a fork.

Stir in the crème fraîche, herbs and seasoning (if using). Serve warm.

# GOOD THINGS

- Cannellini, like most beans, are rich in iron, zinc, magnesium and potassium, and contain a number of phytochemicals that are important for fighting disease.
- Tomatoes are high in the vitamins C and E. They are also rich in antioxidants, which are believed to help fight cancer and heart disease.
- Cheeses, such as Parmesan and Cheddar, are particularly high in iodine, and are good sources of protein.
- Tofu, made from soya beans, is rich in potassium, iron and manganese. Manganese helps to release energy and improve bone strength. Tofu is also a great protein food for vegetarians.

- Cover and refrigerate for no more than 3 days. Not suitable for freezing.

- These dips also make great sauces for pasta dishes.

# Fruit Fingers and Dip

This is a sweet variation on the savoury ideas given on pages 36–8.

**selection of fresh fruit, e.g. apple, banana, kiwi, peach or pear**

**selection of dried fruit, e.g. apricots, mango and apple rings**

Peel and cut the fresh fruit into small fingers, and slice the dried fruit into strips. Serve with one or more sweet dips, such as:
Melted ice cream
Fruit yoghurt or natural yoghurt mixed with honey or jam (Remember: no honey for children under 12 months – see page 18)
Custard
Mashed banana mixed with 1 teaspoon of chocolate spread

# GOOD THINGS

- All fruits are good sources of vitamin C.
- Dried fruits, especially dried apricots, are high in potassium and iron.
- Yoghurt is a good source of calcium and vitamins $B_2$ and $B_{12}$, which improve energy levels and promote growth.

- Refrigerate the fruit for no more than 1 day, and the dips for a maximum of 2 days. Not suitable for freezing.

- Involve toddlers in mixing the melted ice cream and chopping all the softer fruits: they love activities like this.

# Meals

To maximise the amount of healthy food your toddler eats, the recipes in this section should be served with vegetables, such as a few florets of broccoli, some steamed courgettes or strips of carrot. Most veg can be made into finger food, and the greater the variety your toddler tries, the better.

From my own personal experience, if toddlers are given lots of sweet things to eat, they immediately become fussy eaters. For example, the few days following every birthday party that Millie goes to (where the children just run around eating chocolates), she rejects all of her normally favourite dishes.

When food is refused, try not to get cross. When the same food is offered a few days later, toddlers have often changed their minds.

I have also found that if Millie takes part in making a meal, by rolling up meatballs or spring rolls, or chopping and stirring ingredients, she is generally more enthusiastic about eating it.

Mealtimes should always be enjoyable occasions. If young children see you getting pleasure from your food, they are sure to follow suit.

# Mushroom and Spinach Polenta

Although quite bland in itself, polenta (cornmeal) makes a dense bread which can be flavoured with other ingredients to make a very tasty supper dish.

25 g (1 oz) butter
1 small onion, finely chopped
1 garlic clove, crushed
225 g (8 oz) mushrooms, finely chopped
50 g (2 oz) fresh or frozen spinach, finely chopped

80 g (3¾oz) quick-cook polenta
25 g (1 oz) Parmesan cheese, grated
salt and freshly ground black pepper (optional)
oil for greasing

Melt the butter in a frying pan, then add the onion and garlic and cook for 2–3 minutes until softened. Add the mushrooms and cook for another 3 minutes.

Add the spinach and cook for a further few minutes, stirring occasionally. Remove from the heat and set aside.

Bring 350 ml (12 fl oz) water to the boil in a large saucepan. Stirring constantly, pour the polenta in a steady stream into the boiling water. Keep stirring (it gets quite hard) and cook for a few minutes, until the polenta thickens and comes away from the sides of the pan.

Stir in the onion mixture, Parmesan and seasoning (if using).

Oil a 450 g (1 lb) loaf tin, then spoon the mixture into it. Level the surface and tap the sides to remove any air pockets. Leave to cool completely.

When cool, turn out and cut into thick slices. Brush with olive oil and grill for about 5 minutes on each side until golden and crisp.

# GOOD THINGS

- Polenta is made of cornmeal, which is high in iron and carbohydrate.
- Mushrooms are rich in protein and fibre, and are a good source of copper, which promotes growth, helps nerves to work properly and aids in the release of energy.
- Spinach contains a high amount of antioxidants, folic acid and potassium.

- Cover and refrigerate for up to 1 week. Freeze for up to 2 months.

- Slices or fingers of polenta are delicious cold, making them ideal for picnics and travelling.

## Spaghetti Pesto Nests

My toddler loves the stringiness and general messiness of this fun dish. A food-catching bib is highly recommended.

100 g (4 oz) tofu
1 tbsp red or green pesto
2 tsp grated Parmesan cheese
2 tbsp milk

100 g (4 oz) uncooked
  spaghetti, broken in half
150 ml (5 fl oz) milk
2 tbsp olive oil

Place the tofu, pesto, Parmesan and the 2 tablespoons of milk in a food processor or liquidiser and blend to a thick paste.

Cook the spaghetti according to the packet instructions.

Drain the spaghetti, return to the pan and add the 150 ml (5 fl oz) of milk. Place over a low heat and and cook gently for a few minutes, allowing the spaghetti to absorb most of the milk.

Add the pesto and cook gently for another 2–3 minutes. Leave in the saucepan until cool enough to handle – about 10 minutes.

Now take a fork, stick it into the pesto spaghetti and twirl. Stand the forkful of spaghetti upright on a plate, then gently push it off the end of the fork to form a round nest shape. Repeat until the mixture is used up.

Heat the oil in a large frying pan and fry the spaghetti nests for about 3–4 minutes on each side over a medium to high heat, moving them around gently to stop them from sticking.

Drain on kitchen paper and serve when cool enough to hold.

GOOD THINGS

- Pasta is rich in carbohydrate, an important source of fuel and energy.
- Tofu is the perfect protein provider for vegetarians. It promotes tissue formation.

- Cover and refrigerate for up to 2 days. Not suitable for freezing.

- These nests can be eaten cold as an on-the-move food.

# Chicken Nuggets

As a vegetarian, I make these nuggets with Quorn™, but they are popular in any form and are gobbled up much more enthusiastically than the shop-bought variety. The paprika and pepper are gentle introductions to more adventurous tastes for a toddler's palate.

**Makes 10–12 nuggets**

**65 g (2½ oz) breadcrumbs**
**1 tsp cornflour**
**freshly ground black pepper**
**½ tsp paprika**

**225 g (8 oz) skinless chicken or Quorn ™ fillets, cut into pieces about 5 cm (2 in) long and 2.5–4 cm (1–1½ in) wide**
**1 egg, lightly beaten**
**2 tbsp olive oil**

Mix all the dry ingredients together.

Dip the chicken or Quorn ™ pieces into the egg and then into the mixed dry ingredients. Transfer to a plate and, if you have time, leave them to rest in the fridge for about 1 hour to help them become firm.

Heat the oil in a large frying pan until hot but not smoking and fry each nugget for about 3–4 minutes on each side.

Test to make sure the nuggets are properly cooked, and allow to cool a little before serving.

## GOOD THINGS

- Chicken is a good source of iron and of the antioxidant selenium.
- Quorn™, a mycoprotein derived from the mushroom family, is very high in protein, zinc and fibre.

- Cover and refrigerate for up to 3 days. The chicken nuggets are not suitable for freezing, but the Quorn ™ variety can be frozen for up to 3 months.

- Try using large slices of aubergine (pre-fried), beef tomatoes, courgette or sweet potato. Mozzarella and halloumi work well too.

# Fishcakes

These comforting little cakes are very simple to make. The vegetarian variation, using smoked tofu, is a real hit in my house.

**Makes 8**

**225 g (8 oz) white fish, skinned or 225 g (8 oz) smoked tofu**
**300 ml (10 fl oz) milk, for poaching**

**2 medium potatoes, boiled and mashed**
**$\frac{1}{2}$ tsp Dijon mustard**
**small handful chopped fresh parsley**
**flour, for coating**
**oil, for frying**

Preheat the oven to 190°C/375°F/Gas mark 5.

Check that the fish is free of bones, then place in a pan with the milk, bring to a gentle simmer and poach for 3–4 minutes.

Remove the fish, drain on kitchen paper, then flake with a fork.

Mix the mashed potato with the mustard, parsley and fish or tofu. If using tofu, simply mash with a fork. Shape the mixture into 8 even-sized round cakes.

Place a small amount of flour in a bowl and lightly coat the cakes with it.

Heat a little oil in a pan and fry for 2–3 minutes on each side until golden brown.

Transfer the cakes to a greased baking sheet and finish them off in the oven for 10 minutes.

## GOOD THINGS

- White fish is a good low-fat source of protein, vitamins and minerals.
- Potatoes are sources of carbohydrate and fibre.
- Tofu, a form of soya, helps to reduce the risk of free radical damage in the body. (Free radicals are unstable molecules, which are believed to contribute to heart disease and cancer.)

- Cover and refrigerate for up to 2 days. Freeze for up to 2 months.

- These fishcakes are a good way to sneak in vegetables, e.g. peas, sweetcorn and spinach. Other fish can also be used (e.g. tuna or salmon).

# Halloumi with Tomato and Red Lentil Dip

Halloumi is a delicious Greek cheese made from a mixture of sheep's, goat's and cow's milk. It's convenient and simple to prepare, and goes especially well with this dip. Please note however it is not suitable for under ones

1 tbsp olive oil
$\frac{1}{2}$ onion, finely chopped
1 small garlic clove, crushed
$\frac{1}{2}$ red pepper
100 g (4 oz) red split lentils
200g (7 oz) tinned tomatoes
2 tbsp tomato purée
1 tsp mixed dried herbs

450 ml (15 fl oz) salt-free vegetable stock
pinch of sugar (optional)
120 g (4$\frac{1}{2}$oz) halloumi cheese
knob of butter

Heat the olive oil, then gently fry the onion, garlic and red pepper until soft.

Add the lentils, tomatoes, tomato purée and herbs, cover with the stock and bring to the boil. Simmer until the lentils are cooked.

Liquidise in a blender or food processor, adding the sugar if desired.

Slice the halloumi into fingers and gently fry in the butter. Once the juices have evaporated, the cheese browns really quickly, so be careful not to overcook.

Cool a little, then serve the halloumi with a small tub of the red lentil dip.

## GOOD THINGS

- Halloumi is high in protein, calcium and vitamin A.
- Red lentils are a good source of iron and potassium. The latter helps the body to maintain its acid/alkaline balance.
- Tomatoes are rich in antioxidants and potassium.

- Vacuum-packed halloumi keeps for ages, so check the use-by date. It is unsuitable for freezing, but the dip may be frozen for up to 2 months.

- This dip makes a great pasta sauce, especially with added cheese.

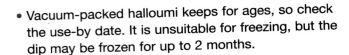

# Tofu Burgers

These cheesy fingers are a soft and crumbly introduction to new tastes and textures.

**Makes about 8 small burgers**

120 g (4½ oz) tofu
1½ tbsp light soy sauce
1 small carrot, grated
1 small garlic clove, crushed

1 slice bread, made into breadcrumbs
1 spring onion, finely chopped
1 egg, beaten
oil, for brushing

Mash the tofu, mix in the soy sauce and leave to marinate for 10 minutes.

Squeeze out any excess liquid, place the tofu in a big bowl and combine with all the other ingredients.

Shape into 8 burgers, then place in the fridge to chill for about 20 minutes.

Lightly brush the burgers with oil and grill under a moderate heat for 8–10 minutes, turning frequently.

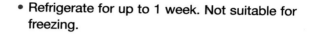

# GOOD THINGS

- The carrot in these burgers provides a useful amount of beta-carotene.
- Garlic contains allicin, which is an antibiotic and an antioxidant known to lower cholesterol and prevent blood clotting.

- Refrigerate for up to 1 week. Not suitable for freezing.

- Any finely chopped vegetable can be used in place of the carrot.

# Lentil Croquettes

Croquettes are perfect finger food, and as these freeze well, they make a quick, easy-to-prepare meal.

175 g (6 oz) green or brown lentils, dried or tinned
1 egg yolk
2 tbsp butter, softened
1 garlic clove, crushed
2 tbsp finely chopped fresh parsley or 1 tsp ground cumin

pinch of salt (optional)
freshly ground black pepper
flour, for dusting
1 egg, beaten
2 slices wholemeal bread, made into crumbs
2 tbsp oil, preferably groundnut, for frying

Cook the lentils according to their packet instructions, then drain and leave to cool. (If using tinned lentils, drain thoroughly.) Put the lentils in a bowl and add the egg yolk, butter, garlic and parsley or cumin. Mix and add the seasoning (if using). Don't worry if the butter is not completely mixed in as the mixture needs to be sticky.

Shape into small sausages, squeezing quite firmly in the palm of your hand. If you have time, leave them to rest in the fridge for 30 minutes.

Dip the croquettes into the flour, then into the egg, and lastly into the breadcrumbs.

Heat the oil in a large frying pan and fry the croquettes in batches, turning occasionally until crisp and golden. Drain on kitchen paper, then cool a little and serve.

## GOOD THINGS

- Lentils are known as a superfood thanks to their high protein and fibre content. They also contain large quantities of iron and B vitamins.
- Garlic is a valuable source of sulphides, which help prevent cancers.

- Refrigerate for up to 1 week. Freeze for up to 3 months.

- These croquettes are delicious served with a dip made of mayonnaise mixed with a little lemon juice.

# Mini Samosas

A delicious and gentle introduction to mild spices, these samosas freeze well, so are a great standby. Simply defrost and reheat in the oven to crispen before serving.

**Makes about 8**

**1 small potato, peeled and cubed**
**1 tbsp oil**
**$\frac{1}{4}$ tbsp cumin seeds**
**$\frac{1}{2}$ small onion, finely chopped**
**$\frac{1}{2}$ tsp mild curry paste**

**50 g (2 oz) finely chopped mixed vegetables, e.g. carrots, green beans, peas and red pepper, or frozen mixed vegetables**
**$\frac{1}{2}$ tbsp lemon juice**
**pinch of salt (optional)**
**2 sheets filo pastry**
**25 g (1 oz) butter, melted**

Preheat the oven to 200°C/400°F/Gas mark 6.

Cook the potato in boiling water until tender, then drain and set aside. Heat the oil and gently fry the cumin seeds for 3 minutes.

Add the onion and fry over a medium heat for about 5 minutes.

Stir in the curry paste and cook for a further minute, before adding the potato, vegetables, lemon juice and salt (if using). Mix well.

Cut each sheet of filo into 4 strips. Place a heaped tablespoon of mixture at the top of each strip. Fold one corner of the filo over the filling to make a triangle. Then fold the triangle over and over in alternate directions until the pastry strip is used up and you have a neat triangular parcel.

Place the samosas on a greased baking sheet, brush with the melted butter and bake for 5–6 minutes until crisp and golden.

## GOOD THINGS

- Lots of vitamins and minerals are provided by the mixed vegetables.

- Refrigerate for up to 3 days. Freeze for up to 3 months.

- This is a great recipe for using up lots of tired-looking vegetables.

## Meatballs

These freeze brilliantly and are really handy as a quick-fix dinner.

**Makes about 16**

**450 g (1 lb) beef, lamb or chicken mince**
**1 slice bread, made into breadcrumbs**
**1 small red onion, finely chopped**

**1 tbsp tomato purée, sundried or regular**
**1 garlic clove, finely chopped**
**1 tsp mixed dried herbs**
**salt and freshly ground black pepper**

Mix all the ingredients together by hand or in a food processor.

Roll into balls a bit bigger than a walnut. (At this point, put any meatballs surplus to requirements in the freezer.)

Preheat the grill to a moderately high heat.

Place the meatballs on a baking sheet, spaced about 2.5 cm (1 in) apart and grill for 12–14 minutes, turning halfway through the cooking time.

Test before serving to ensure that the meat is thoroughly cooked.

## GOOD THINGS

- The meat in this recipe provides a good dose of protein, iron, zinc and B vitamins.
- Garlic contains the antibiotic allicin, which is an antioxidant known to lower cholesterol and prevent blood clotting.

- Refrigerate for up to 1 week. Freeze for up to 3 months.

- Try serving these meatballs with Italian tomato sauce (see page 56) and pasta, rice or mashed potato.

# Vegetarian Meatballs

These yummy meatballs are very popular – and not just with vegetarians.
Try them and see.

**Makes about 16**

1 tbsp olive oil
1 small red onion, finely
  chopped
1 garlic clove, finely chopped
200 g (7 oz) vegetarian (soya or
  Quorn ™) mince
1 tsp dried mixed herbs

1 tbsp tomato purée, sundried
  or regular
1 tbsp passata or tinned
  chopped tomatoes
1½ slices of bread, made into
  breadcrumbs
1 egg, beaten
freshly ground black pepper

Preheat the oven to 200°C/400°F/Gas mark 6.

Heat the oil and fry the onion and garlic for 3–4 minutes, until soft.

Add the mince, together with the herbs, tomato purée and passata, and cook for a further 5 minutes. Stir in the breadcrumbs, then remove from the heat.

Cool to room temperature before mixing in the egg.

Using your hands, mould the mixture tightly into walnut-sized balls. (At this point you can freeze any that are surplus to requirements.)

Place the balls on a greased baking sheet and bake for 20 minutes until browned.

# GOOD THINGS

- Vegetarian mince, like tofu, provides your toddler with protein and all the benefits of soya (see page 38).
- Tomato purée and passata are rich in lycopene, an antioxidant known to help prevent heart disease and cancer. It is more potent in processed tomatoes than fresh ones.

- Refrigerate for up to 1 week. Freeze for up to 3 months. (Cook from frozen at 200°C/400°F/Gas mark 6 for 30 minutes.)

- These meatballs are delicious served with Italian tomato sauce (see page 56) and with mashed potato, spaghetti or rice.
- For a change, try serving the meatballs in a pitta bread with salad.

# Italian Tomato Sauce

This sauce has so many uses: it's great for serving with meatballs and pasta, for spreading on the base of home-made pizza, or for using as a warm dip.

olive oil, for frying
1 small red onion, chopped
1 garlic clove, finely chopped
400 g (14 oz) tin chopped
  tomatoes
1 tbsp tomato purée

$\frac{1}{2}$ tsp dried mixed Italian herbs
splash of balsamic vinegar
salt and freshly ground black
  pepper (optional)
small handful fresh basil
  (optional)

Heat a little oil in a medium-sized saucepan.

Add the onion and fry gently for 3 minutes. Add the garlic and fry for another minute.

Add all the remaining ingredients, apart from the basil, and cook slowly on a low heat for about 20 minutes, stirring occasionally.

If using basil, tear up the leaves and add now.

Serve the sauce chunky, or blend until smooth in a liquidiser.

# GOOD THINGS

- Tomatoes are a top source of potassium, crucial for muscle and nerve functions in the body.

- Cover and refrigerate for up to 1 week. Freeze for up to 12 months.

- Ring the changes with this recipe by adding any chopped cooked vegetables, tuna or chicken you have to hand, and serve with pasta or rice.

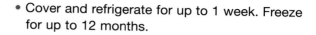

# Potato Cake Faces

Children relish things in recognisable shapes, and funny faces always seem to be especially popular.

**Makes about 6**

**300 g (11 oz) potatoes, peeled and cut into large chunks**

**$1\frac{1}{2}$ tbsp milk**
**knob of butter**
**50 g (2 oz) Cheddar cheese, grated**

Preheat the oven to 190°C/375°F/Gas mark 5.
  Boil the potatoes until cooked (about 15 minutes).
  Add the milk and the butter to the strained potatoes and mash thoroughly.
  Mix in the grated cheese and leave to cool slightly.
  Roll a chunk of the mash to about the size of a golf ball and flatten

into a circle about 1 cm ($\frac{1}{3}$ in) thick.

Mark out eyes, nose and mouth with a skewer or sharp knife. You could use peas for the eyes, carrot for the nose and red pepper for the mouth. Basically, anything goes.

Place the faces on a greased baking sheet and bake in the oven for about 10 minutes until they begin to brown.

## GOOD THINGS

- Potatoes are a good source of vitamin C and fibre.
- Cheddar and all hard cheeses are great sources of calcium, which is especially important during the early years for bone growth.

- Refrigerate for up to 1 week. The unbaked mixture can be frozen for up to 3 months.

- Try adding some finely diced cooked vegetables or lentils to the basic potato mixture – a sneaky way of serving more goodness to reluctant vegetable eaters.

58

# Burrito Wraps

Toddlers love helping to fill and roll these burritos. The tomato filling goes really well with the sour cream and cheese.

**Makes 3**

**75 g (3 oz) mixed vegetables, e.g. 2 mushrooms, 4 green beans and 1 small carrot**
**50 g (2 oz) kidney beans, cooked**
**knob of butter**
**½ small onion, chopped**

**1 tbsp olive oil**
**3 tbsp passata**
**150 ml (5 fl oz) salt-free vegetable stock**
**3 flour tortillas**
**3 tsp soured cream**
**grated Cheddar cheese, for sprinkling**

Preheat the oven to 180°C/350°F/Gas mark 4.

Finely chop the mixed vegetables and lightly crush the kidney beans.

Heat the butter and fry the onion until soft, then add the vegetables, kidney beans and the olive oil.

Gently fry for about 4 minutes before adding the passata and stock. Simmer for a further 5 minutes until the mixture has thickened.

Meanwhile, wrap the tortillas in foil and warm in the preheated oven for about 5 minutes.

Place a generous teaspoon of the vegetable mixture in the centre of each tortilla, adding a teaspoon of sour cream and a sprinkling of cheese on top.

Fold in the sides, then roll into neat packages and serve.

## GOOD THINGS

- Tortillas are a good source of energy and some vitamins (enriched flour only) but unleavened ones contain a greater variety of vitamins and minerals
- Kidney beans are high in iron, potassium and complex carbohydrates.
- The vegetables are a good source of beta-carotene, vitamin C and fibre.

- Refrigerate for up to 1 week. Freeze the vegetable mixture only for up to 3 months. (Sour cream does not freeze.)

- Serve with chicken or Quorn ™ pieces for an even more substantial meal.

## Schnitzels

Traditionally a veal recipe from Austria, toddlers love the softness of the meat, contrasted with the crunchy breadcrumbs. They're great for dipping too.

**Makes about 8**

75 g (3 oz) pork escalope
50 g (2 oz) breadcrumbs

about 100 g (4 oz) plain flour
1 egg, beaten
oil, for frying

Cut the pork into bite-size chunks.

Put the breadcrumbs, flour and egg into separate bowls. Dip each piece of pork into the flour, then the egg and finally into the breadcrumbs.

Heat a little oil in a frying pan and then fry the schnitzels for 2–3 minutes on each side until golden and cooked through. Drain on kitchen paper and serve.

# GOOD THINGS

- Pork is a good source of protein, essential for growth of muscles and tissue.
- Tofu (used in the vegetarian option below) is made from soya beans, one of the few plant sources of complete protein.

- Cover and refrigerate for up to 2 days. Not suitable for freezing.

- For a vegetarian option, substitute 1 packet of tofu for the pork. Cut into slices about 1cm ($\frac{1}{3}$in) thick, pat dry and gently fry in 2 tbsp light soy sauce and 1 tbsp olive oil for 3–4 minutes. Coat and cook as described in the meat method above.

# Savoury Pancakes

Toddlers love watching these being made and then helping to fill and roll them up. I always find that Millie eats more if she feels she has participated in the preparation.

**100 g (4 oz) plain or wholemeal flour**
**pinch of salt (optional)**
**1 egg**

**300 ml ($\frac{1}{2}$ pint) milk**
**1 tbsp oil**
**oil, for frying**

Sift the flour and salt (if using) into a bowl. If using wholemeal flour, return the bran to the bowl after sifting.

Make a well in the flour, break in the egg and add a little milk. Stir gently.

Gradually mix in the rest of the milk and the tablespoon of oil until the mixture has the thickness of single cream.

Cover and refrigerate for at least 20 minutes before using. (The batter can be kept in the fridge for up to 1 day.)

Heat a medium frying pan, then brush with a little oil. Pour a small amount of batter into the pan and swirl around to cover the base, the thinner the better.

Cook for about a minute or until the edges are coming away from the sides of the pan and it starts to bubble up from underneath. Flip the pancake over and cook for another minute until golden in colour. Transfer to a plate, cover with greaseproof paper and keep warm. (Putting greaseproof paper between the pancakes will stop them sticking together.)

Repeat until all the batter has been used.

Divide your chosen filling (see pages 64-65) between the pancakes, then roll up each one, tucking in the sides as you go to hold in the filling.

GOOD THINGS

- White flour is a good source of calcium and carbohydrate.
- Eggs are a good source of protein, vitamin A & D. Milk is a good source of protein and calcium but remember that cow's milk should not be given as a drink to children under the age of one.

- Refrigerate for up to 3 days. Freeze for up to 6 months.

- The pancakes can be made up to a day ahead (or frozen) and warmed in the oven before serving.

# Savoury Pancake Fillings

Pancakes can be filled with absolutely anything.
Here are a couple of suggestions that I hope are as popular
with your toddler as with mine.

## Spinach in A Cheesy Sauce

**2 handfuls fresh spinach
or 50 g (2 oz) frozen
25 g (1 oz) butter
40 g (1½ oz) plain flour
250 ml (8 fl oz) milk,
warmed but not boiled**

**40 g (1½ oz) medium or
mature Cheddar cheese,
grated
salt and freshly ground
black pepper to taste
(optional)**

Wash the fresh spinach, shake well, then place in a pan over a low heat
and allow to wilt. Alternatively, heat the frozen spinach until defrosted.
Drain well and set aside.

Melt the butter in a medium-sized saucepan, then add the flour and
stir briskly over the heat for 1 minute.

Add a little drop of the milk to form a paste, then gradually add the
rest of the milk, stirring all the time until the mixture thickens. If it gets
lumpy, whisk vigorously.

Cook the sauce over a gentle heat for a few minutes, stirring slowly.
Add the spinach and grated cheese. Season as required.

# Mushroom, Bacon and Tomato Sauce

**knob of butter**
**100 g (4 oz) mushrooms, finely chopped**

**2 rashers lean bacon or 4 slices vegetarian bacon, chopped into small pieces**
**2 medium tomatoes, finely chopped**

Melt the butter in a small saucepan, add the mushrooms, and cook for 2–3 minutes.

Add the bacon and cook over a medium heat until it starts to crispen.

Add the tomatoes, stir well, then turn the heat to low and cook for a good 5 minutes until the mixture resembles a thick sauce.

GOOD THINGS

- Spinach and tomatoes are the top two sources of potassium, crucial for the muscle and nerve functions of the body.
- Bacon is high in protein and a source of zinc, an immune system booster.

- Refrigerate for up to 2 days. Freeze for up to 3 months.

- Just about anything can be added to these sauces, including ham, lentils and tuna. These sauces can also be used with pasta.

# Savoury Filo Parcels

These crispy delights are really easy to make, and toddlers love the experience of biting into the noisy pastry.

**Makes 4 of each filling**

**4 sheets filo pastry**
**25 g (1 oz) butter, melted**

Ricotta and spinach filling
**100 g (4 oz) spinach, fresh or**
**frozen**
**knob of butter**
**120 g ($4\frac{1}{2}$ oz) ricotta cheese**
Red pepper and feta filling
**$1\frac{1}{2}$ tbsp olive oil**
**$\frac{1}{2}$ red pepper, finely chopped**
**65 g ($2\frac{1}{2}$ oz) feta cheese,**
**finely chopped**

Preheat the oven to 190°C/375°F/Gas mark 5.

Start by making the ricotta and spinach filling. If using fresh spinach, wash well and shake off the excess moisture. Place in a covered pan, cook gently until wilted, then drain. If using frozen spinach, cook until defrosted. Transfer to a sieve and squeeze out any excess moisture.

Melt the butter in the pan, add the spinach and stir in the ricotta.

To make the red pepper and feta filling, gently heat the oil in a pan and cook the pepper for a couple of minutes until softened. Take the pan off the heat, add the feta and mix well.

To make the parcels, lay out 2 sheets of filo pastry one on top of the other and cut into four equal rectangles. Put a generous tablespoon of filling in the centre of each top sheet.

Gather up the pastry corners and twist or pinch together to enclose the filling. If you prefer, roll into a sausage shape and pinch the ends together.

Place the parcels on a greased baking sheet and brush with the melted butter.

Bake for 10 minutes until lightly browned and crisp.

Cool slightly before serving as the centres can be very hot.

# GOOD THINGS

- Red peppers are known as a superfood thanks to their high levels of beta-carotene and vitamin C.
- Spinach also contains vitamin C.
- Feta and ricotta cheeses are good sources of calcium and vitamin A.

- Refrigerate for up to 2 days. Not suitable for freezing.

- The parcel fillings can be varied in any way you like. Why not try using bacon, tuna or lentils? The feta can be replaced with Cheddar.

# Mini Spring Rolls

These are much easier to make than you might think, and as they freeze well, it's worth making a big batch.

**Makes 10**

**25 g (1 oz) fine rice noodles or vermicelli**
**3 tbsp sunflower, groundnut or vegetable oil**
**50 g (2 oz) carrot, cut into small dice**
**50 g (2 oz) mangetout, cut into small dice**
**1 tsp fresh root ginger, grated**

**25 g (1 oz) spinach, fresh or frozen**
**2 tbsp light soy sauce**
**1 tbsp chopped fresh mint**
**1 tbsp chopped fresh coriander freshly ground black pepper, to taste**
**5 sheets filo pastry**
**egg white**
**oil, for frying**

Soak the noodles according to the packet instructions, then drain and rinse, as they do tend to stick. Cut into 2.5 cm (1 in) lengths.

Heat the oil in a wok or large frying pan and fry the carrot, mangetout and ginger for a few minutes.

Stir in the spinach (washed and shaken dry if fresh, defrosted if frozen), plus the soy sauce, herbs, pepper and noodles. Leave to cool slightly. Lay the pastry out one sheet at a time, keeping the other sheets under a damp tea towel to stop them drying out.

Cut each sheet into two long, thin rectangles. Brush with a little egg white. Place a tablespoonful of the mixture towards one end of the pastry. Roll up gently, tucking in the sides as you go. Repeat this process with the remaining pastry and filling.

When all the spring rolls are ready, either fry them in a little oil (they do taste nicer fried), or bake for 15 minutes at 200°C/400°F/Gas mark 6. Leave to cool slightly before serving, as they can be very hot inside.

# GOOD THINGS

- Spinach is a good source of betacarotene which is converted into vitamin A in our bodies and also contains vitamin C.
- The carrot in these spring rolls also provides betacarotene, which is a valuable antioxidant and is essential for healthy vision, skin and growth.

- Refrigerate in a sealed container for up to 1 week. Uncooked rolls may be frozen for up to 12 months.

- Use peas, spring onions or sweetcorn instead of the mangetout.
- If you have no fresh herbs to hand, use 1 tsp of each dried variety.
- Vary the quantity of root ginger, depending on how adventurous your toddler is.
- Root ginger, once peeled, can be frozen and chopped or grated when needed.

# Mini Pizzas

Children love adding the toppings to pizzas, and seem much more inclined to gobble them up if the topping ingredients are arranged into faces or patterns. If you don't have time to make your own dough, use a packet of shop-bought pizza dough mix, or ready-made mini pizza bases.

Dough
**225 g (8 oz) strong plain flour**
**½ tsp salt**
**½ tsp fast-action dried yeast**
**120 ml (4 fl oz) warm water**
**1½ tbsp olive oil**
Toppings
**base spread, such as Italian tomato sauce (see page 56), tomato purée, pesto, olive paste or passata**

**any of the following:**
**grated cheese, mozzarella cubes, bacon, chopped ham, finely chopped tuna, pineapple, sliced sausages (meat or vegetarian), mushrooms, chopped cooked spinach with an egg broken in the middle, sweetcorn, finely chopped courgette**

Preheat the oven to about 220°C/425°F/Gas mark 7.

Sift the flour and salt into a bowl and stir in the yeast.

Make a well in the centre and gradually work in the water and oil to form a dough.

Knead the dough on a lightly floured surface for 6–8 minutes until smooth and elastic.

Place in an oiled bowl and turn the dough over once to coat the surface with oil. Cover with clingfilm and leave to rise in a warm place for about 1 hour, until roughly doubled in size.

Once risen, turn out the dough and knead again for a few minutes.

Roll out the dough to a thickness of 1 cm ($\frac{1}{3}$ in), then cut into circles of the size you want.

Load up the pizza toppings.

Bake the pizzas on greased baking sheets for 7–15 minutes, according to their size.

## GOOD THINGS

• Cheese is high in protein and calcium – great for children's teeth and bones.

• Refrigerate for up to 3 days. The uncooked bases can be frozen for up to 3 months.

• For a different texture, use muffins or French bread for the pizza bases.

# Risotto Fingers

These are what I would term 'comfort food'. They are also a great way of using up leftover rice or risotto.

**Makes about 10**

**knob of butter**
**1 small red onion, finely chopped**
**½ red pepper, finely chopped**
**100 g (4 oz) risotto rice**

**375 ml (13 fl oz) hot salt-free vegetable stock**
**1½ tbsp grated Parmesan cheese**
**flour, for coating**
**1 egg, beaten**
**100 g (4 oz) breadcrumbs**
**oil, for frying**

Melt the butter in a pan and fry the onion and pepper gently over a low heat until soft – about 5 minutes.

Add the rice, mix well and stir over the heat for about 2 minutes.

Over a low to medium heat, add the stock little by little. Allow the rice to absorb the liquid before you add the next ladleful.

Keep stirring until all the liquid has been absorbed. This should take about 25 minutes. Don't worry about overcooking; the mixture is better if it's on the sticky side.

Leave to cool for a few minutes, then stir in the Parmesan.

Pat the mixture into small sausage shapes, then dip them first in the flour, then the egg and finally the breadcrumbs.

Shallow-fry in a little oil over a medium to high heat for a few minutes on each side until crisp.

Drain on kitchen paper and allow to cool a little before serving.

# GOOD THINGS

- Rice is a low-fat carbohydrate food, a good source of lasting energy.
- Onions, contain substances called organosulphides which seem to stimulate the immune system, helping to fight of infections like colds and flu
- The Parmesan and egg are good sources of vitamin B$^{12}$, essential for growth and helping to maintain the health of the body's nerves and cells.

- Refrigerate for up to 1 day. Not suitable for freezing.

- Vegetables can be used in place of the rice; try small florets of broccoli, diced carrots, mushrooms, peas, spinach or sweetcorn.

## Savoury Puff Pastry Tarts

These are very quick to prepare and always popular. Decorating them with faces goes down well, too.

**Makes 8 individual tarts
(4 of each filling)**

**175 g (6 oz) ready-made puff
pastry**
**1 egg, beaten**

Mushroom filling
**knob of butter, for frying**
**150 g (5 oz) mushrooms, finely
chopped**
Tomato filling
**8 cherry tomatoes, finely sliced
red pesto or olive paste
olive oil**

73

Preheat the oven to 190°C/375°F/Gas mark 5.

Roll out the pastry until it is about 1 cm (⅓in) thick.

Using an 8 cm (3 in) cutter, cut out circles of pastry and transfer them to a greased baking sheet. Score another circle inside each one using a 5 cm (2 in) cutter. (Take care not to cut right through the pastry.) Prick the inner circles gently with a fork, then set aside.

For the mushroom filling, melt the butter in a frying pan and gently cook the mushrooms for a few minutes until softened.

Spoon the mushrooms into 4 inner circles of pastry.

Brush the outer rim of the pastry with beaten egg.

For the tomato filling, spread 4 inner circles of pastry with a little red pesto or olive paste, then lay slices of tomato on top and drizzle with a little olive oil.

Bake the tarts for 6–7 minutes.

## GOOD THINGS

- Puff pastry is high in carbohydrate and fat, good energy providers for an active toddler.
- Mushrooms are high in protein and fibre.

- Refrigerate for up to 3 days. Freeze for up to 6 months.

- Anything can be used as a filling for these tarts. Tuna mixed with a little crème fraîche works well.

# Mini Calzone

These pizza turnovers are exciting for toddlers – their very own parcels to bite into and explore. If you don't have time to make your own dough, you could use a packet of shop-bought pizza dough mix.

**Makes 4**

Dough
**225 g (8 oz) strong plain flour**
**½ tsp salt (optional)**
**½ tsp fast-action dried yeast**
**120 ml (4 fl oz) warm water**
**1 tbsp olive oil**
Filling
**2 tbsp olive oil**
**1 garlic clove, crushed**

**1 medium red onion, finely chopped**
**½ tsp chopped rosemary**
**½ tsp grated lemon zest**
**50 g (2 oz) mozzarella cheese, diced**
**75 g (3 oz) ricotta cheese**
**1 tsp red pesto or olive paste**
**salt and freshly ground black pepper**

Make the dough (see page 70), then leave to rise. (This takes around 15 minutes' preparation and 1 hour's rising time.)

Heat the oil and gently fry the garlic for 1 minute, then add the red onion. Cook for a further 2 minutes before adding the rosemary and the lemon zest.

Gently cook for a further 5 minutes until the onion has softened and browned. Turn into a bowl and leave to cool.

When cool, add the mozzarella, ricotta and red pesto or olive paste to the onion mixture. Season to taste. Turn the oven to 220°C/425°F/Gas mark 7 and heat a greased baking sheet. Knead the dough, then divide it into four equal portions. Roll each portion into a circle about 15 cm (6 in) in diameter.

Spoon the filling into one half of each circle.

Dampen the edges of the dough with a little water, then fold over and press together to create half-moon shapes.

Place the calzone on the heated baking sheet on the top shelf of the oven and bake for about 10 minutes, until golden.

Leave to stand for 5 minutes before serving.

# GOOD THINGS

- Cheese is one of the few good sources of vitamin $B_2$.
- A great way to enrich your toddler's diet is with lots of nutritious toppings such as bacon, tuna or other vegetables.

- Refrigerate for up to 2 days. Uncooked calzone may be frozen for up to 3 months.

- Try halving the size of the circles to make eight tiny calzone.

# Stuffed Baby Tomatoes

Toddlers find these colourful tomatoes so pretty and enticing that they need no coaxing to eat them. They also very much enjoy helping to stuff them with the couscous filling.

25 g (1 oz) couscous
100 ml (3 ½ fl oz) salt-free
   vegetable stock

12 cherry tomatoes
25 g (1 oz) feta cheese, finely
   chopped

Preheat the oven to 190°C/375°F/Gas mark 5.

Put the couscous in a bowl and pour the stock over it. Stir once, then cover and leave to stand for about 5 minutes until all the liquid has been absorbed.

Slice the top off each tomato. Scoop out the pulp and add it, along with the feta cheese, to the couscous. Mix well.

Carefully fill each tomato with the couscous mixture and place on a baking sheet or mini muffin tray (the latter helps them to hold their shape).

Bake for about 5 minutes, until the tomatoes are slightly browned and the cheese is starting to melt.

# GOOD THINGS

- Tomatoes are considered a superfood because they are high in lycopene, an antioxidant known to reduce the risk of heart disease and cancer. They are also rich in vitamins C and E.
- Feta cheese provides a good dose of calcium, and its vitamin $B_{12}$ content helps to promote growth.

- Refrigerate for up to 3 days. Not suitable for freezing.

- These also work well with mushrooms, stalks removed, stuffed and cooked as above.

# Snacks

I have such strong memories of that mid-afternoon hunger I experienced as a child – usually after a morning of non-stop running around, but at its most intense after swimming. The recipes in this chapter offer ideas for quick and nutritious snacks that will satisfy even the most energetic toddler.

Snacks should be sufficient to fill a hole but not affect your toddler's appetite for main meals. And making them yourself ensures that they don't contain any artificial additives, such as flavourings, preservatives or colourings.

Snacks are a life-saver after a busy day at the nursery, at home or out and about. Whether eaten in a home-made den or in the kitchen with a warm drink on a rainy day, the snacks below will fill those gaps between breakfast, lunch and dinner in a healthy and delicious way.

# Vegetable Crisps

These are really easy to make and so much healthier than shop-bought crisps. They are delicious grilled with a pile of grated cheese on top and served with sour cream.

**150 g (5 oz) assorted vegetables, e.g. beetroot, butternut squash, carrot, celeriac, green beans,** **parsnip, potato, pumpkin, sweet potato**
**can of spray oil**

Preheat the oven to 220°C/425°F/Gas mark 6.

Wash all the vegetables and peel those that need it. Slice all of them very thinly using a vegetable peeler.

Spray some oil onto a couple of baking sheets and brush them to make sure they are well covered. Heat the baking sheets for about 5 minutes in the oven.

Place the vegetable slices on the baking sheets, taking care not to overlap them. Lightly spray with oil.

Cook in the oven for 6–7 minutes, turning halfway through. When ready, they should look crisp and golden.

Remove the crisps from the baking sheets and place on kitchen paper. Eat as soon as they are cool enough.

## GOOD THINGS

- Orange-fleshed vegetables, such as butternut squash, carrot and sweet potato, are rich in carotenes and other antioxidants, which are essential for cell protection.
- Oil sprays coat utensils and food very lightly, so you use much less and the result is healthier.

- Store in an airtight container for 3–4 days. Not suitable for freezing.

- While still hot, toss the crisps with some herbs, paprika or finely grated Parmesan. These crisps served with dips (see pages 30–7 ) make a substantial snack or a complete light lunch.

# Cubes

These fun little cubes introduce your baby to different textures and tastes.

**butter**
**1 slice wholemeal bread**
**honey or fruit spread**
   **(Remember: no honey for**
   **children under 12 months**
   **– see page 18)**
**1 pitta bread**
**dash of olive oil**
**accompaniments, peeled and**
**cubed as necessary, e.g.**
**apple, pear, carrot, red and**
**yellow pepper, sausage, thin**
**salami, ham or chicken**
**hard cheeses, e.g. Cheddar,**
**Edam, Gruyère, Jarlsberg**

Preheat the oven to 150°C/300°F/Gas mark 2.

Butter the bread lightly on both sides, then spread either honey or fruit spread on one side.

Brush the pitta with a little olive oil.

Cut the bread and the pitta into cubes and place them in the oven for 30 minutes, or until dried out.

Offer only a small selection of accompaniments with the bread and pitta cubes.

## GOOD THINGS

- Hard cheeses are great sources of calcium and are also high in phosphorus, essential for strong bones and teeth.
- Wholemeal bread supplies a good amount of fibre, as well as many other vitamins and minerals.

- Store in an airtight container for up to 1 day. Not suitable for freezing.

- To make croutons, brush the bread with a little olive oil instead of spreading with butter.

## Eggy Bread

This makes a great breakfast, lunch, pudding, supper or snack: a truly versatile and quick fallback finger food. It's even more appreciated if cut into fun shapes.

**knob of butter**
**2 eggs, beaten**

**1 tbsp milk or cream**
**2 slices bread**

Whisk the eggs with the milk or cream in a large bowl.
Soak the bread into the mixture for a few minutes, until saturated.
Fry gently in the butter until brown and crispy. Cut into fingers and serve.

## Savoury variations
- Make a sandwich, then dip it in the egg mixture and fry. Fillings that work well include butter and Marmite, and hard cheese, such as Cheddar. (Please note: Marmite is not suitable for under ones)

## Sweet variations
- Treat the eggy bread as brioche and cover with chocolate spread.
- Try drizzling maple syrup or honey over the eggy bread.

### GOOD THINGS

- Bread is a good source of carbohydrate and if wholemeal bread is used, a good source of fibre as well.
- Eggs are a good source of Iron and vitamins A and $B_2$.
- If using cheese, cheese provides energy and also calcium for growing bones.

- Eat immediately. Not suitable for freezing.

- The savoury variations are delicious served with ketchup or mayonnaise.

# Sweetcorn on the Cob

This is a novelty food in its own right, popular with all toddlers:
Millie adored it from an early age.

**1 corn cob**          **knob of butter**          **1 tbsp honey**

Remove the husk and silky threads from the corn, cut off the ends if
necessary, then snap or cut into small pieces.

Place in a large pan of boiling water and simmer for about 10 minutes
or until tender.

Melt the butter with the honey in a frying pan. Once sizzling, add the
chunks of corn and gently fry until slightly browned.

Cool a little before serving.

## GOOD THINGS

• Sweetcorn is high in fibre and vitamin C.
• Butter is high in fat – a useful calorie boost for growing toddlers.
• Honey is a good natural alternative to sugar.

• Cover and refrigerate for up to 3 days. Not suitable
  for freezing.

• Corn on the cob is perfect on-the-move food too
  – kids love it hot or cold.

# Dried Fruit Toffee Sticks

These might look like something you give to a dog, but don't be put off: my toddler absolutely adores them. These sticks are very useful on car journeys as they don't create too much mess.

**200 g (7 oz) soft dried fruit, e.g. apple rings, apricots, berries, cherries, dates, peaches,** **prunes and raisins (avoid anything too dry or with tough bits)**

Preheat the oven to 100°C/200°F/Gas mark $\frac{1}{4}$.
Line a baking sheet with baking parchment.
Whiz the dried fruits in a blender until they form a lumpy paste.
Mould into thin fingers and place on the lined baking sheet.
Bake in the centre of the oven for 2 hours, or until slightly hardened.
(They will still be quite chewy.)

# GOOD THINGS

- Dried fruits, especially apricots, are a very good source of iron.
- Containing only natural sugars, these sticks are much healthier than shop-bought sweets.

- Store in an airtight container at room temperature up to the use-by date on the dried fruit packets.

- These sticks are delicious dipped in melted plain chocolate (as are most dried fruits).

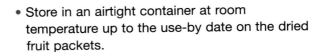

# Oat Biscuits

These biscuits make a lovely teatime treat, and as they are such good energy boosters, they're perfect for on-the-move snacks too.

**100 g (4 oz) wholemeal flour**
**25 g (1 oz) porridge oats**
**½ tsp baking powder**

**pinch of salt (optional)**
**2 tbsp golden syrup**
**50 g (2 oz) butter**

Preheat the oven to 180°C/350°F/Gas mark 4.

Mix all the dry ingredients in a bowl, then stir in the syrup.

Rub in the butter using your fingers to form a soft dough.

Flour the work surface, place the dough on it and pat into a flat shape about 5 mm (¼ in) thick.

Use an 8 cm (3 in) cutter to cut out the biscuits.

Lightly grease a baking sheet, place the biscuits on it and bake for about 10 minutes until they are slightly browned. Leave to stand for 5 minutes before cooling on a wire rack.

# GOOD THINGS

- Wholemeal flour contains lots of fibre and carbohydrate, and is a good source of magnesium, which is essential for strong bones and teeth.
- Oats are rich in fibre and a great source of energy.

- Store in an airtight container at room temperature for up to 1 week. Freeze for up to 6 months.

- As an extra treat, why not add some chopped dried fruit, raisins or chocolate chips to the basic dough mix?
- These biscuits go perfectly with a cup of warm or cold milk.

# Teatime Biscuits

Baking is a great activity for little children, making them appreciate real food from a very early age and promoting their creativity and independence. Millie loves making these biscuits, and they taste good despite being cut out in mad messy shapes and having three raisin eyes.

**Makes about 30**

**225 g (8 oz) plain flour**
**pinch of salt (optional)**
**100 g (4 oz) butter**
**3 tbsp golden caster sugar**
**1 egg yolk, beaten**

**1–2 tbsp cold water**
Icing
**100 g (4 oz) icing sugar**
**1 tsp lemon juice**
**1–2 tbsp water**
**tiny drop of food colouring**
  **(optional)**

Sift the flour and salt (if using) into a mixing bowl. Rub in the butter by hand or with a mixer until the mixture resembles breadcrumbs.

Stir in the sugar and beaten egg, adding enough water to make a soft dough.

Wrap the dough in clingfilm and put in the fridge for 20–30 minutes. Preheat the oven to 180°C/350°F/Gas mark 4.

Roll out the dough to a thickness of 1 cm ($\frac{1}{3}$ in) and cut into shapes using the cutter of your choice. Re-roll the scraps and continue cutting until all the pastry has been used.

Lightly grease a baking sheet, place the pastry shapes on it and cook for 8–10 minutes, until golden in colour. Cool on a wire rack.

For the icing, sift the icing sugar and mix with the lemon juice, adding just enough water to make a thick but spreadable paste. Stir in the food colouring, if using.

Place a small amount of icing on each biscuit and smooth with the back of a warm teaspoon.

**Variations**

Add 25 g (1 oz) of chocolate drops or currants to the basic dough mixture to make choc chip or fruit biscuits.

After smoothing on the icing, decorate with raisins or chocolate buttons.

# GOOD THINGS

- There's lots of energy provided in the ingredients of these biscuits – perfect for teatime hunger.
- Being additive-free and low in sugar, these biscuits are much healthier than shop-bought ones.

- Store in an airtight container for up to 1 week. The uncooked dough can be frozen for up to 6 months.

- Add a pinch of cinnamon or ginger to the basic mixture and skewer a hole in the top of each biscuit before baking to make Christmas decorations.

# Food On The Move

The dreaded journey by car, train, plane or boat… Every parent worries about keeping toddlers happy and healthy during long trips. I have found that things seem to go more smoothly if routines are abandoned somewhat, but that needn't mean plying children with chocolate buttons and packets of crisps to keep them quiet.

Snacks are the name of the game: substantial finger food at normal mealtimes and nibbles at other times. Making sure your baby or toddler has enough to drink is important too, so no-spill cups are a blessing.

## Useful things to pack
- Carrier bags for rubbish
- Food-catching bibs
- Baby wipes for hands and faces
- Food bags and clips
- In-car bottle warmer that plugs into the lighter
- No-spill cups
- Plastic bowls/plates with sections
- Tea towels for covering legs while eating
- Plastic tubs for leftovers
- Cool box for cold storage

## Good things to eat
- Peeled boiled eggs (quails' eggs are a great novelty if you are feeling generous)
- Cherry tomatoes
- Crudités (e.g. raw carrot, celery, courgette, red pepper, cut into strips)
- Small tub of dip (see pages 30–7)
- Peeled and cubed fruit (see page 80)
- Mini box of raisins
- Bananas
- Bagged-up home-made crisps (see page 79)
- Breadsticks and cheese straws (see pages 24 and 27)
- Mini-cartons of juice with straws

Travelling with babies and toddlers is never going to be plain sailing but the following recipes will take some of the strain out of feeding en route.

Bon voyage!

# Sausage Rolls

No party is complete without sausage rolls, but they are also ideal for taking on picnics or outings.

**50 g (2 oz) dry sage and onion stuffing mix**
**250 g (9 oz) sausagemeat or ½ 150 g (5 oz) packet**

**Sosmix, made to the packet instructions up to the point of cooking**
**200 g (7 oz) puff pastry**
**1 egg, beaten**

Preheat the oven to 200°C/400°F/Gas mark 6.

Sprinkle the sage and onion stuffing mix onto your work surface and place the sausagemeat on top. Pat and roll into a sausage shape about 50 cm (20 in) long, fully coating it with the stuffing.

Roll the pastry into a rectangle measuring approximately 50 x 15 cm (20 x 6 in).

Place the sausage on the pastry. Brush beaten egg along one long edge of the pastry about 1 cm (⅓in) from the edge. Fold the pastry over the sausage and press the edges together firmly.

Brush the remaining beaten egg over the surface of the pastry, then cut the roll into approximately 20 slices. Make a 1 cm (⅓in) slit on top of each roll.

Dampen the surface of a large baking sheet and place the sausage rolls on it.

Bake for 10-12 minutes until golden brown. Allow to cool before serving.

## GOOD THINGS

- Although sausagemeat has a high fat content, this is not a problem for toddlers as they use up so much energy.
- Sosmix is made from textured vegetable protein, which has a protein content similar to that in sausagemeat, but a much lower fat content.
- Puff pastry is also high in carbohydrate and fat, making these sausage rolls a great source of energy overall.

- Refrigerate in an airtight container for up to 3 days. Freeze for up to 3 months.

- Before freezing puff pastry, cut it into portions so that you can use a small quantity each time.

## Tortilla Fingers

This recipe makes a big tortilla (enough to feed a family), but it doesn't really matter, as it will soon be devoured.

**2 medium potatoes, peeled and cut into 1 cm (⅓in) cubes**
**large knob of butter**
**1 small onion, finely chopped**
**2 tbsp double cream or milk**
**pinch of grated nutmeg**

**freshly ground black pepper**
**pinch of salt (optional)**
**6 eggs, beaten**
**2 tbsp grated cheese, such as Parmesan, Cheddar or Gruyère**

Boil the potatoes until just tender, then drain and set aside.

Melt the butter in a 20 cm (8 in) frying pan and gently cook the onion until softened.

Add the potato and gently fry for 5 minutes, stirring continuously.

Stir the cream or milk, nutmeg and seasoning (if using) to the beaten eggs and pour on top of the onion and potato mixture. Leave on a low heat for a few minutes until almost set. (The top should remain a little runny at this stage.)

Preheat the grill until moderately hot.

Sprinkle the cheese on top of the tortilla and place under the grill in the frying pan until lightly browned and set.

Turn out onto a large dinner plate, cut into fingers and serve (or pack for your outing).

**Variations**

Anything can be added to this tortilla, e.g. mushrooms, spinach, mixed vegetables, tuna chunks, ham, bacon, cheese or herbs, so it's a great way of adding extra ingredients that your toddler might otherwise reject.

GOOD THINGS

- Eggs provide a good dose of protein.
- Potatoes have a high carbohydrate content – a good source of energy.

- Refrigerate for up to 3 days. Not suitable for freezing.

- Spoon the partly cooked tortilla mixture into a bun tin or muffin tray before grilling to make mini portions.

# Mini Quiches

I make these in a mini muffin tray and freeze them. They're really useful as a quick meal, and the 'baby quiches' (as Millie calls them) are a real winner with toddlers, who adore all things tiny. You can use ready-made pastry if you don't want to make your own.

**Makes about 16, or 9 if using a regular size muffin tray**

Pastry
**120 g (4½oz) plain flour**
**pinch of salt**
**65 g (2½oz) butter, softened**
**1–2 tbsp cold water**

Filling
**25 g (1 oz) butter**
**25 g (1 oz) flour**
**150 ml (5 fl oz) milk, slightly warmed**
**2 eggs, beaten**
**salt and freshly ground black pepper (optional)**
**50 g (2 oz) mature Cheddar cheese, grated**

Preheat the oven to 190°C/375°F/Gas mark 5.

Start by making the pastry. Sift the flour into a bowl, add the salt, then rub in the butter until the mixture resembles breadcrumbs. Add the water a little at a time until a dough has formed. Shape into a ball and cool in the fridge for 30 minutes.

Meanwhile, make the filling. Melt the butter over a gentle heat. Stir in the flour and cook for 1 minute.

Stirring constantly, gradually add the milk, a little at a time, until a thick sauce forms. Leave to cool for a few minutes, then whisk in the eggs. If desired, season with salt and pepper.

Lightly grease the muffin tray.

Roll out the pastry to a thickness of about 5 mm (¼in). Using an 8 cm

(3 in) cutter (or a mug of similar diameter), cut the pastry into circles. Gently press a pastry circle into each hole of the tray.

Put a little grated cheese into the base of each pastry case, then spoon the egg mixture on top.

Bake for about 10 minutes, until risen and starting to brown.

Leave in the tin for a few minutes before cooling on a wire rack.

**Variations**

To ring the changes, extra ingredients can be added after the eggs have been whisked in. Try mushrooms cooked in a little butter, cooked lentils, cooked fresh or frozen spinach seasoned with a little nutmeg, cubed ham, sliced bacon or tuna.

- Cheddar cheese provides a healthy dose of chromium, which controls the level of sugar in the blood.
- Eggs are rich in vitamin A, essential for strengthening the immune system.

- Refrigerate for up to 3 days. Freeze for up to 3 months.

- If making pastry, why not double the quantities, divide into small portions and freeze for future use?

# Tubs of Goodies

These are fun for little fingers to delve into, and particularly useful for journeys and picnics. If you don't have any tubs, you could use little plastic cups or beakers covered with clingfilm, or sandwich bags fastened with wire ties.

**Fills 2 little tubs**

**dried fruit selection, e.g. raisins, sultanas, currants, berries, dates, apricots, banana crisps, apple rings, mango**

**fresh fruit selection, e.g. grapes, satsuma segments, cherries, physalis oddments, e.g. cheese, cherry tomatoes, broken bits of biscuit, cereal (Shreddies or Cheerios – nothing too flaky)**

Chop all the large dried fruit into small pieces and mix with the other ingredients.

Fill your chosen containers.

# GOOD THINGS

- This mixture is much healthier and more exciting than crisps.
- Dried fruits, especially apricots, are a very good source of iron.
- Although tempting, **don't** add nuts for children under 5 as they're a choking hazard.

- Store in an airtight container for a few days. Not suitable for freezing.

- As a big treat, you could add chocolate drops (white and dark for variety).

# Cornish Pasties

These make a substantial on-the-move meal. You can make different sizes for different-sized stomachs – big for Daddy, tiny for Baby. Use shop-bought pastry if you don't want to make your own.

**Makes 4–5 large or 8–10 small pasties**

Pastry
**200 g (7 oz) plain or wholemeal flour**
**pinch of salt (optional)**
**75 g (3 oz) butter, softened**
**cold water**
Filling
**120 g (41/2 oz) good-quality mince, or cubed steak or chicken, or vegetarian mince**

**1 tsp dried mixed herbs**
**3 tbsp passata**
**1 medium onion, sliced**
**1 small potato, peeled and cubed**
**75 g (3 oz) swede, peeled and cubed**
**1/4 tsp salt (optional)**
**1 tbsp olive oil**
Topping
**25 g (1 oz) butter**
**milk or a little beaten egg, for brushing**

Preheat the oven to 220°C/425°F/Gas mark 7.

Place the flour and salt (if using) in a bowl, then rub in the butter until the mixture resembles breadcrumbs. Mix in enough cold water to make a dough. Chill in the fridge for 30 minutes.

If making the meat filling, combine all the ingredients in a bowl. (There's no need to pre-cook them.) If making the vegetarian option, cook all the ingredients, including the cubed vegetables, in the olive oil, stirring over a gentle heat for about 5 minutes. Flour the work surface and roll out the pastry to about 5 mm ($\frac{1}{4}$ in) thick. Cut out 4–5 circles 15 cm (6 in) in diameter (a saucer is a good guide for this), or 8–10 circles 8 cm (3 in) in diameter (use a mug).

Divide the filling between the pastry circles, and put a tiny knob of butter on top of each portion. Dampen the edges of the pastry with water and fold over to make a semicircle. Crimp the edges with a fork and brush the pasties with a little egg or milk to help them brown. Place on a baking sheet and bake for 10 minutes. Turn the temperature down to 180°C/350°F/Gas mark 4 and bake for a further 20 minutes.

## GOOD THINGS

- Beef is rich in iron and a good source of zinc.
- Swede contains valuable antioxidants and also is high in fibre.

- Refrigerate for up to 3 days. Freeze for up to 3 months.

- Any chopped root vegetables can be used in place of the swede.

# Cheesy Wholemeal Scones

These are best warm from the oven, but they are also delicious cold, and make invaluable travelling companions.

**Makes 6 large or 12 small scones**

**100 g (4 oz) self-raising flour**
**50 g (2 oz) plain or wholemeal flour**
**½ tsp baking powder**

**½ tsp mustard powder**
**½ tsp salt (optional)**
**25 g (1 oz) butter, softened**
**100 g (4 oz) Cheddar cheese, grated**
**1 egg**
**2–3 tbsp milk**

Preheat the oven to 200°C/400°F/Gas mark 6.

Mix the flours, baking powder, mustard and salt (if using) in a large bowl.

Rub in the butter with your fingers until the mixture resembles breadcrumbs. Add 75 g (3 oz) of the grated cheese and mix.

In a separate bowl, mix the egg and 2 tablespoons of milk. Add this to the flour mixture and combine to make a dough, adding a little more milk if too dry.

Flour the work surface and roll out the dough to a thickness of about 2 cm (¾in). Use an 8 cm (3 in) cutter for large scones or a 5 cm (2 in) cutter for smaller ones. (Alternatively, to save time, simply mould the dough into a cake shape and cut into slices.)

Put the scones onto a greased baking sheet. Brush the top of each with milk, then sprinkle with the remaining cheese.
Bake for about 10 minutes, until risen and golden.

## GOOD THINGS

- Cheese is a good source of vitamins $B^2$ and $B^{12}$ (essential for vegetarians for preventing anaemia).
- Wholemeal flour is a great source of fibre.
- Full of carbohydrate, these scones give an energy boost.

- Store in an airtight container at room temperature for up to 1 week. Freeze for up to 6 months.

- These scones are great dipped in soup as a main meal, or filled like sandwiches for meals on the move.

# Sandwich Fillings

To make a change from the usual fillings, here are a
few suggestions that are popular with my toddler and her friends. Each
recipe makes enough for one round of sandwiches (2 slices of bread).

## Bacon, Lettuce and Tomato
Cook a rasher of bacon until crispy and chop into small pieces. Mix
with some chopped tomato and 1 tablespoon of mayonnaise.

## Carrot, Cream Cheese and Peanut Butter
Spread 1 slice of bread with smooth peanut butter and the other with
cream cheese. Top one half with grated carrot, then sandwich the slices
together.

## Creamy Mexican Bean
Stir 1 tablespoon of sour cream into 2 tablespoons of mixed cooked
beans. (You could use canned beans in a spicy Mexican sauce or
refried beans.)

## Coronation Chicken
Take enough cooked chicken to fill a sandwich and mix with 1
tablespoonful each of mayonnaise, plain yoghurt, sultanas and $\frac{1}{4}$
teaspoon of mild curry paste.

# GOOD THINGS

- Bacon is a good source of zinc (vital for healthy growth in children) and B vitamins.
- Peanut butter is the top source of biotin, essential for storing energy in our bodies.
- Beans are high in a wealth of vitamins and minerals, including zinc, iron and B vitamins to name but a few.
- Chicken, whole grain and dairy products contain selenium, an antioxidant necessary for healthy skin, muscles and healthy heart function.

- These fillings keep for up to 1 day in the fridge. None is suitable for freezing.

- Vegetarian bacon may be substituted for the genuine article in a BLT and Quorn ™ fillets can replace the meat in coronation chicken.

# Sweet Treats

Some people believe that sugar should be avoided at all times. With the best of intentions I tried to do so, but birthday parties, child-minders and grandparents, along with my own desire to 'treat' my toddler and indulge the enjoyment she experienced from eating chocolate and cake, eventually made me cave in. I still try to keep sweet things as treats, being only too aware of how much sugar children today consume and how little good it does them.

There are many advantages to making your own treats, the main one being that you can ensure they are free of additives. Another pleasure is that they are great for parent and child to make together (making fairy cakes and biscuits is our favourite rainy day activity), and, of course, you get to eat them warm.

The recipes on the following pages each make enough for a family tea. After all, better to have too many cakes than too few.

# Chocolate Brownies

It's impossible to overstate how popular a treat these are. They make a lovely pudding, too.

**100 g (4 oz) butter**
**50 g (2 oz) cocoa powder**
**2 eggs**
**225 g (8 oz) caster sugar**

**1 tsp vanilla essence**
**50 g (2 oz) self-raising flour**
**50 g (2 oz) chocolate chips**

Preheat the oven to 180°C/350°F/Gas mark 4.

Take a shallow baking tin, approximately 23 cm (9 in) square, and line it with baking parchment.

Melt the butter, then add the cocoa powder, stirring well to remove any lumps. Beat the eggs in a large bowl. Add the sugar and mix until smooth. Stir in the cocoa mixture and the vanilla essence.

Gradually add the flour, stirring until everything is fully combined.

Mix in the chocolate chips. Pour the mixture into the lined baking tin and place in the middle of the oven for about 30 minutes. When done, the brownies should be crisp on top and soft in the middle.

Leave to cool for 10 minutes before cutting into squares.

# GOOD THINGS

- Chocolate, although best as a rare treat, is a source of calcium, and the cocoa contains iron and antioxidants.
- These brownies are calorific and very filling – a good instant remedy for urgent hunger pangs.

- Refrigerate in an airtight container for up to 1 week. Freeze for up to 6 months; defrost before reheating in the oven.

- Add chopped fruit or raisins instead of chocolate chips to make the brownies slightly healthier.

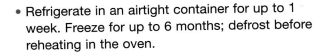

## Chocolate - Dipped Fruit

Outrageously delicious, these treats are a great way to make toddlers eat fruits they would normally reject.

**250 g (9 oz) fruit, e.g. peach, apple, strawberries, kiwi and pineapple**

**100 g (4 oz) plain chocolate (milk chocolate and white chocolate work less well)**

Wash all the fruit. Hull the strawberries and peel other fruit as appropriate.

Carefully remove any pips or stones and cut the flesh into segments.

Pat dry with kitchen paper (essential to ensure the chocolate sticks well).

Place a heatproof bowl over a pan of boiling water, making sure it does not actually touch the water. Break up the chocolate, place in the bowl and allow to melt completely.

Spread a sheet of greaseproof paper on your work surface.

Using a fork, dip each piece of fruit into the melted chocolate, shaking off the excess before placing on the greaseproof paper to harden. When all the fruit has been dipped, place in the fridge until the chocolate is fully set.

## GOOD THINGS

- All fruit is high in vitamin C.
- Pineapple contains the enzyme bromelain, which helps digestion by aiding the breakdown of protein.

- Best freshly prepared. Not suitable for freezing.

- Satsuma and orange segments, plums, mango, papaya, banana and apricots all work well too.

## Flapjacks

Although very sweet, flapjacks are wholesome teatime treats, providing plenty of fibre.

**Makes about 12**

**100 g (4 oz) butter or margarine**

**100 g (4 oz) demerara sugar**
**1 tbsp golden syrup**
**150 g (5 oz) porridge oats**

Preheat the oven to 160°C/325°F/Gas mark 3.
   Grease a baking tin or loaf tin approximately 18 cm (7 in) square.
   Melt the butter in a pan, then stir in the sugar, syrup and oats.
   Turn the mixture into the prepared baking tin and press flat using the back of a metal spoon.

Bake in the oven for about 35 minutes, or until golden brown.
Leave to cool for about 10 minutes, then mark out 12 squares.
Cool completely before removing the flapjacks from the tin.

**GOOD THINGS**

- Oats are considered a superfood because they are very high in fibre and have a low glycaemic index. This means that the carbohydrate and glucose they contain are absorbed slowly into the body, thus providing long-lasting energy.
- Being additive-free and containing only the most natural ingredients, these home-made flapjacks make a much healthier treat than the shop-bought variety.

- Store in airtight container at room temperature for up to 1 week. Freeze for up to 6 months.

- Liven up the basic recipe by adding 25 g (1 oz) of chopped dried apricots or chocolate chips.

# Mini Muffins

These dinky muffins are just the right size for little hands to hold. Although 24 might seem like a lot, they go so fast that it's worth making a large number.

**Makes 24 mini muffins (or 12 regular size)**

**75 g (3 oz) butter**
**200 g (7 oz) plain flour**
**2¼ tsp baking powder**
**75 g (3 oz) caster sugar**

**pinch of salt (optional)**
**1 egg**
**100 g (4 oz) plain yoghurt**
**100 ml (3½ fl oz) semi-skimmed milk**
**150 g (5 oz) fresh blueberries or 75 g (3 oz) dried blueberries**

Preheat the oven to 200°C/400°F/Gas mark 4.

Place paper cases in a 24-hole mini muffin tray or a 12-hole large muffin tray.

Melt the butter and leave to cool.

Mix all the dry ingredients in a bowl.

In a separate bowl, combine the egg, yoghurt and milk with the melted butter.

Pour the wet ingredients into the dry, stirring with a metal spoon. (Do not overmix – it should look a little lumpy.)

Fold in the blueberries and spoon the mixture into the paper cases.

Bake for 12–15 minutes, until the muffins have risen and are golden in colour. (Large muffins will take around 20 minutes.)

## GOOD THINGS

- Blueberries contain a powerful antioxidant.
- The milk and yoghurt, provide calcium for strong bones and healthy teeth.
- This recipe contains only about half the amount of sugar found in a shop-bought cake, making it a much healthier option.

- Best eaten as quickly as possible while fresh. Freeze for up to 3 months.

- Sliced apple, banana and pear, chocolate chips, raisins and desiccated coconut can be substituted for the blueberries.

## Fruit Pizzas

This recipe is a good way of getting toddlers interested in fruit. If you don't have time to make your own dough, you could use a packet of pizza dough mix.

**Makes 4**

Dough
**1/2 tsp fast-action yeast**
**120 ml (4 fl oz) warm water**
**250 g (9 oz) plain flour**
**¼ tsp salt (optional)**
**¼ tsp sugar**

Topping
**sliced fresh fruits, e.g. apple
(with a sprinkling of
cinnamon), apricot, banana,
cherries, grapes, mango,
peach, pear, plums,
strawberries
raisins, for sprinkling
4 tsp caster sugar**

In a large bowl, stir the yeast into the water. Add the flour, salt (if using) and sugar, and mix to form a dough.

Knead for about 5 minutes, then place in a bowl and cover with clingfilm. Leave to rise in a warm place for at least 1 hour, until doubled in size.

Once risen, knock the air out of the dough and cut into four equal pieces.

Preheat the oven to 220°C/400°F/Gas mark 6.

Roll out each piece of dough into a circle measuring about 15 cm (6 in) in diameter and place side by side on a greased baking sheet.

Arrange a layer of fresh fruit on each pizza, scatter a few raisins on top and sprinkle with a teaspoon of sugar.

Bake for 10–15 minutes, until the dough is crisp and the fruit is starting to caramelise.

Cool slightly, then serve with a little extra sugar if needed.

## GOOD THINGS

- The dough provides carbohydrate, which is essential for energy.
- Any fruit will give your toddler a good quantities of minerals and vitamins.

- Refrigerate for up to 2 days. The uncooked bases can be frozen for up to 3 months.

- For a real treat, put chocolate spread on the pizza base before adding the fruit.

# Healthy Banana Cakes

These easy-to-make cakes are free of added sugar, yet children still seem to love them.

**Makes 12 fairy cakes or 24 tiny petit four cakes**

90 g (3½oz) butter, softened
2 ripe bananas, mashed
1 egg, beaten
85 ml (3 fl oz) milk
1 tbsp runny honey
200 g (7oz) self-raising
   wholemeal flour

¼ tsp baking powder
90 g (3½oz) sultanas
Icing
120 g (4½oz) cream cheese
1 tbsp runny honey
1 tsp lemon or orange juice
   (optional)

Preheat the oven to 180°C/350°F/Gas mark 4.
   Line your bun tray with the appropriate size and number of paper cake cases.
   Cream together the butter and bananas.
   Mix in the egg, milk and honey.
   Gently fold in the flour, baking powder and sultanas.
   Divide the mixture between the paper cases, then place in the oven and bake for about 15 minutes, until they are golden in colour.
   Cool on a wire rack before decorating.
   To make the icing, mix all ingredients together to a smooth paste and spread a little on each cake.

# GOOD THINGS

- Honey is a good source of energy. It is also said that eating honey from your local area helps the body to develop a resistance to the local pollen, and therefore to hay fever.
- Sultanas are a good source of energy.

- Store in an airtight container for up to 5 days. Not suitable for freezing.

- Use dried fruit to make faces on the icing: raisins for eyes, cherries for the nose, apricots for the mouth.

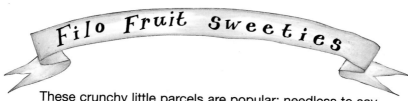

# Filo Fruit Sweeties

These crunchy little parcels are popular; needless to say, the chocolate ones are the favourites.

**Makes 3 sweeties per filling recipe**

**4 sheets filo pastry**
**25 g (1 oz) butter**

Chocolate and
   strawberry filling
**6 strawberries, finely chopped**
**3 heaped tsp chocolate spread**
Peach and mascarpone
   filling
**½ peach, finely chopped**
**2 tbsp mascarpone cheese**
**1 tsp honey**

Preheat the oven to 180°C/350°F/Gas mark 4.

Place one sheet of filo pastry on top of another and cut into 3 equal rectangles.

In separate bowls, mix the ingredients together for each filling recipe.

Put a good spoonful of filling at the top of each rectangle.

Wet the edges of the pastry and roll into a sausage. Twist the ends so that each roll looks like a wrapped sweet.

Place on a greased baking sheet and brush with the melted butter.

Bake for about 10 minutes, or until browned.

Cool before serving, as the contents can be really hot.

## GOOD THINGS

- Filo is the healthiest pastry you can use, as it contains hardly any fat.
- Strawberries are an excellent source of vitamin C, and contain ellagic acid, which is believed to fight cancer.
- Mascarpone is a good source of carbohydrate and vitamins A and $B_{12}$.

- Refrigerate for up to 1 day before cooking. Not suitable for freezing.

- Any fruit, fresh or dried, can be added to these sweeties.

# Banana Fritters

These fritters are crunchy and warming. Don't be put off by the deep-frying– they're worth it.

**Makes 8**

50 g (2 oz) plain flour
pinch of salt
$\frac{1}{2}$ tbsp sunflower oil
50 ml (2 fl oz) milk
25 ml (1 fl oz) water

1 egg
oil, for deep-frying
2 bananas, halved lengthways
 and across
icing sugar, for sprinkling
 (optional)

Sift the flour and salt into a bowl. Pour in the sunflower oil, milk and water and beat well. Add the egg and beat again. Heat the oil in a large saucepan until it starts to smoke. Dip the banana pieces into the batter. Allow the excess to drip off, then carefully lower into the oil.

Fry the fritters in several batches, until brown and crisp.

When ready, remove from the pan and drain on kitchen paper. Once all the pieces have been fried, sprinkle a little icing sugar over them (if desired), and serve when cool enough to hold.

# GOOD THINGS

- Bananas are a good energy food. They are also rich in potassium, which is vital for the healthy functioning of muscles and nerves.
- Sunflower oil is a top provider of vitamin E, essential for the maintenance of the skin, heart, nerves, muscles and blood circulation.

- Eat fresh and hot. Not suitable for freezing.

- These fritters are fabulous dipped into softened ice cream or plain yoghurt.

# Ice Lollies

These summertime treats are a much healthier alternative to additive-packed commercial lollies. You will need lolly moulds to make them.

## Stripy ice lollies

**150 ml (5 fl oz) light-coloured fruit juice, e.g. apple, mango or other naturally sweet varieties**

**150 ml (5 fl oz) dark-coloured fruit juice, e.g. grape, cranberry, blackcurrant or raspberry**

Pour light and dark juice alternately into the lolly moulds, freezing between each addition for about 30 minutes or until solid. Repeat until the moulds are full.

You could, of course, fill the whole lolly mould with just one juice to save time, but the plain-coloured lollies don't seem to be adored in quite the same way as the stripy variety.

## Yoghurt lollies

**175 g (6 oz) strawberries**
**150 g (5 oz) Greek yoghurt**

**1 ½ tsp honey**
**dash of vanilla essence**

Purée all the ingredients in a blender until smooth, then pour into lolly moulds. Freeze until solid.

## Fresh fruit purée lollies

**300 ml (10 fl oz) puréed fruit,**

**e.g. apple, mango, melon, peach, pear**

Pour the purée into the moulds and freeze until solid.

**GOOD THINGS**

- Fruit juices are a great way to give your toddler a quick fix of vitamin C and all the other benefits that fruits possess.
- Yoghurt gives your toddler calcium, as well as the vitamins $B_2$ and $B_{12}$.

- Freeze for up to 3 months.

- In the yoghurt lollies, the strawberries can be replaced with mango, peach, plum or raspberry purée.
- If your child is happy to eat more textured lollies, you could try adding small chunks of soft chopped fruit, such as mango or peach, to the basic fruit purée.
- Ice lollies can be useful teething soothers for your toddler.

# Jam Tarts

A classic teatime treat for children. These tarts are very easy to make, especially if using ready-made shortcrust pastry, and toddlers love helping to spoon in the jam.

**Makes 12**

**225 g (8 oz) plain flour**
**pinch of salt (optional)**
**100 g (4 oz) butter**

**1 $\frac{1}{2}$ tbsp caster sugar**
**1 egg yolk, beaten**
**1–2 tbsp cold water**
**strawberry, apricot or**
**raspberry jam**

Pastry can be made either in a food processor or by hand. Either way, start by mixing the flour and salt (if using), then rub in the butter to make a mixture resembling breadcrumbs.

Add the sugar and beaten egg, then slowly mix in enough water to make a soft dough.

Wrap the ball of dough in clingfilm and refrigerate for about 30 minutes.

Preheat the oven to 200°C/400°F/Gas mark 6.

On a lightly floured surface, roll out the pastry to about 1.5 cm (1/2 in) thick.

Using an 8 cm (3 in) fluted biscuit cutter (or mug of similar size), cut out circles of pastry and press them gently into a greased bun tin.

Spoon the jam into the pastry cases, being careful not to overfill them.

Decorate the tops with pastry shapes, such as hearts, flowers or stars. Bake for about 15 minutes, then leave to cool on a wire rack.

## GOOD THINGS

- While jam tarts aren't exactly health food, they do provide plenty of calories for energy, and the eggs and butter in the pastry are good sources of vitamins A and D.

- Store in an airtight container at room temperature for up to 1 week. Freeze for up to 6 months.

- Try mixing cubed pieces of real fruit with the jam. Raspberry, strawberry, pear and peach work well.

## Fairy Cakes

Fun to make and decorate, fairy cakes are always firm favourites at teatime.

**Makes about 12**

**100 g (4 oz) self-raising flour**
**1 tsp baking powder**
**100 g (4 oz) caster sugar**
**100 g (4 oz) soft margarine**
**2 eggs**

Icing
**75 g (3 oz) icing sugar**
**1 tbsp lemon juice**
**water or food colouring**

Preheat the oven to 200°C/400°F/Gas mark 6.

Line a bun tray with 12 paper cases.

Put all the cake ingredients into a large mixing bowl and beat well for 3–4 minutes.

Divide the mixture between the paper cases, then bake in the oven for 15 minutes, until the cakes are risen and golden.

Remove from the oven and leave to stand for a minute or so before placing on a wire rack to cool.

Meanwhile, sift the icing sugar into a bowl. Add the lemon juice and a drop of water or food colouring and mix to a smooth consistency. Spread a little icing on top of each cake when cold and decorate as you please.

## GOOD THINGS

- The margarine contains polyunsaturates and/or monosaturated fats, a healthier option than the saturated fat in butter.
- The eggs provide iron and a good dose of vitamin B$_{12}$, essential for promoting growth and maintaining a healthy nervous system.

- Store in an airtight container at room temperature for up to 1 week. Freeze for up to 6 months.

- Add 25 g (1 oz) currants and ½ teaspoon lemon zest to the basic fairy cake mixture.
- Fairy cakes are particularly irresistible if made in tiny petit four cases.

# Index